THINK B!G

BRIAN TRACY

THINK B!G

For an **Extra**ordinary Life

Published 2026 by Gildan Media LLC
aka G&D Media
www.GandDmedia.com

THINK BIG. Copyright © 2026 by Brian Tracy. All rights reserved.

No part of this book may be used, reproduced or transmitted in any manner whatsoever, by any means (electronic, photocopying, recording, or otherwise), without the prior written permission of the author, except in the case of brief quotations embodied in critical articles and reviews. No liability is assumed with respect to the use of the information contained within. Although every precaution has been taken, the author and publisher assume no liability for errors or omissions. Neither is any liability assumed for damages resulting from the use of the information contained herein.

Front cover design by David Rheinhardt of Pyrographx

Interior design by Meghan Day Healey of Story Horse, LLC

Library of Congress Cataloging-in-Publication Data is available upon request

ISBN: 978-1-7225-0724-4

10 9 8 7 6 5 4 3 2 1

Contents

Introduction 7

one   Goal Setting and the Psychology of Success   13
two   Commit to Excellence   31
three   Harness Your Unlimited Thinking Power   55
four   You Are a Genius   73
five   The Keys to Wealth Building   93
six   The Power of Decision   111
seven   Possibility Thinking   129
eight   Bouncing Back from Defeat   149
nine   Creative Networking   167
ten   Character Makes the Difference   187
eleven   Developing Personal Power   205
twelve   The Keys to Success   225

Introduction

We have entered into the greatest period in human history. Wherever you are and whatever you may be doing, there have never been more opportunities for you to achieve your goals and aspirations than exist around you right now.

Economists say that we are entering into the golden age of mankind. We have passed from the material world into the mental world, into the Psychozoic Age, the age of the mind. Wealth and opportunities are contained in the person you are and the way you think rather than in the things you have acquired or the situation you find yourself in.

Because all wealth is essentially mental, there are no limits on how much of it you can acquire. In this book, I'll explain a series of simple, practical, proven methods, techniques, and strategies used by all high-achieving men and women in every field to accomplish far more than they or the people around them have ever dreamed possible. I'll show you how to break the bonds of limited conventional thinking and expand your mind and your ambitions to the point where you can greatly exceed any goal that you've ever set for yourself.

Three major forces are ripping through our world today: the incredible growth in information, technology, and competition. They are dramatically transforming everything they touch, creating unlimited opportunities for the creative minority.

The information revolution, combined with the speed of information processing, is causing knowledge in every field to double every two to three years. Fully 90 percent of all the thinkers, inventors, engineers, scientists, writers, entrepreneurs, and creators of all kinds are living and working today. The results of their efforts are becoming almost instantaneously available to one another, thereby doubling and tripling their outputs. The explosion in technology and high-speed computers is breathtaking. Today you can email a message around the world to thousands of people simultaneously in a matter of seconds. The Internet gives you access to tens of millions of people online, as well as to the recorded knowledge stored in more than tens of thousands of libraries and research institutes. Instantaneous transmission of data enables the money markets to move $1 trillion per day, sometimes in seconds, making it virtually impossible for countries to control their currencies anymore, much less their economies.

We have already seen the astonishing transformation wrought by the introduction of the smartphone in 2007. You almost certainly have a smartphone, but you may not know exactly what it is. Here is a definition from the TechTarget website: "a cellular telephone with an integrated computer and other features not originally associated with telephones, such as an operating system (OS), web browsing and the ability to run software applications." You hold in your pocket a supercomputer that far exceeds the capacities of computers that only a few decades ago took enormous rooms to hold. This device enables you to communicate instantaneously with almost anyone almost anywhere in the world. As of early 2024, it has been estimated that there are 6.84 billion smartphones—astonishing, given that the current world population is estimated at 8 billion.

The third major factor driving our lives is competition. Every individual and every company wants to be successful in the worldwide marketplace. To be successful, they must be continually coming up with faster, better, newer, cheaper, and easier ways to deliver value to their customers. Every advance in knowledge and technology creates opportunities that fleet-footed competitors can run with to create new products and services and leapfrog one another in global markets. The current proliferation of artificial intelligence (AI) has already had a startling impact. In 2022, 19 percent of Americans were in jobs that were regarded as most vulnerable to developments in AI, and it is estimated that as many as 60 percent of new jobs will be affected by AI integration.

Some will find these facts alarming, but the good news is that every single change opens up more opportunities and possibilities to achieve your goals and make progress faster than ever before.

The ancient Greek philosopher Heraclitus said, "Everything is in flux": everything changes. The biggest single factor in your life today is change, affecting everything you do, and it is accelerating week by week and month by month. You have no control or choice over this process: you only have to decide whether or not you are going to be a master of change or a victim of it. Are you going to be a creator of circumstances or a creature of circumstances? Are you going to ride the wave and stay ahead of the curve of change, or are you going to be bowled over by it and left in its wake? It'll be one or the other, but the impact of change will be forced upon you whatever you do.

You are always free to choose. The only limits on what you can do, have, and be are the limits that you accept on your abilities and your own potential. By learning how to think big about yourself and your future, you will learn how to take firm control over the direction of your life and accomplish more in the next few years than most people might accomplish in a lifetime.

At the outset, let me tell you a little bit about my own background. Back in the sixties, I left high school without graduating. I traveled and worked at laboring jobs for a few years before I stumbled into sales. In sales, I spun my wheels for many months until I finally had a breakthrough that changed my life: I realized that all the top salespeople around me seemed to have selling skills that enabled them to prospect, present, follow up, and close sales far faster and easier than me. So I went to one of the top salespeople and asked him what he was doing differently that enabled him to make so many sales and earn so much money, and he told me. When I began following his advice, prospects reacted to me differently, and my sales started to go up.

I began asking other top salespeople for advice, I began following it, and my sales went up even further. I read books on selling in the morning and tried out the new ideas during the day, I listened to audio programs in my car and carried an audiocassette player around with me between calls. I began going to sales training seminars and taking careful notes, and each time my sales increased. Soon I was one of the top salespeople. I went from a boarding house to a beautifully furnished apartment and from taking buses and taxis to having my own car. Soon I was flying around the world in jets, eating in fine restaurants, and staying at

Introduction

first-class hotels. I learned this amazingly important lesson: you can learn anything you need to learn to accomplish any goal you can set for yourself. This is not an easy rule, but it is simple. You too can learn anything you need to accomplish any goal you can set for yourself.

> You can learn anything you need to learn to accomplish any goal you can set for yourself.

With this idea in mind, I changed jobs and industries. I got into real estate, sales, and leasing, and then into real estate development. Then I got into importation and distribution and then banking, printing, advertising, consulting, and eventually training and speaking.

Every time I got into a new field, I learned everything I possibly could about that field and applied it as fast as I could. At first, I checked out all the books from the local library. Then I bought my own books and built my own library. I listened to every audiocassette and attended every seminar. In my thirties, I went back and took a business degree at a university so I could understand microeconomic theory, statistics, probability management, science, and accounting. I studied marketing, management, administration, and strategic planning. I became addicted to learning. It changed my life.

But the most astonishing thing was that when I looked around me, I noticed that very few other people were doing what I was doing. Most people, by their own admission, were living lives of quiet desperation. They were working at jobs they didn't particularly like, earning salaries far below their potentials, staying in relationships they didn't enjoy, and living lives that gave them no great satisfaction. I tried to tell them that the only way out was up. I told anyone who would listen that they could learn anything they needed to learn to achieve any goal they could set; there were no limits. But few people seemed to listen.

Everything happens for a reason. If you can find the reasons why other people succeed in any field and you do the same things, you can get the same results if you stick to it long enough and work hard enough. When I found that the people around me didn't seem to be interested in changing their situations, I began looking for the reasons underlying their behavior, and I found them. I will set them out in this book.

one

Goal Setting and the Psychology of Success

Many years have gone into researching the psychology of success and failure, and most of the studies conclude that there are two major mental blocks that hold people back. The first is what Dr. Martin Seligman of the University of Pennsylvania has called "learned helplessness." According to his research, this attitude afflicts 80 percent of the population—perhaps more. People feel helpless. People feel overwhelmed by so many things going on around them. They feel that there is nothing they can do to improve their lives. The predominant signal that learned helplessness has set in is contained in the words "I can't." People feel that they can't lose weight, can't get a better job, can't improve or change their relationships, can't increase their incomes, can't upgrade their knowledge and skills, and can't do anything else that they really want to. They have tried unsuccessfully so many times in the past that they have concluded that they can do nothing to change the future. So they get up in the morning, go to work, come home at night, and watch television for four or five hours before wandering off to bed.

The second malady that holds people back is the *comfort zone.* Human beings are creatures of habit. They begin doing something and soon become comfortable with it. After a while, they become extremely reluctant to change what they're doing or the situation they're in, even if they're not particularly happy or satisfied with it. They become content and complacent and eventually they become afraid to change for any reason. They get into a rut, and the longer they stay in it, the deeper it grows until they finally lose all hope of ever changing or improving their lives.

The deadly combination of learned helplessness and the comfort zone leaves a person feeling trapped and helpless, weak and powerless, unable to take control or to make any real difference in their lives.

But the truth is that there are no real limits on what you can accomplish with your life.

Whatever anyone else has done, you can probably do as well. The very fact that you can set a clear goal for yourself means that you probably have the ability to achieve it. In fact, if you think back, you'll recall that you eventually got anything that you ever really wanted long enough and hard enough. You are not helpless, and you are not stuck in a rut or a comfort zone, except by choice. Your true potential is limited only by your own imagination.

You are not helpless except by choice.

The Two Forms of Blockage

The two factors that create the feeling of helplessness and of being stuck in a rut are fear and ignorance. Fear is and always has been your greatest enemy. Fear and self-doubt do more to hold you back from big dreams and great accomplishments than any other factors. And the less you know about a subject, the more fearful you are of embarking on something new, better or different.

This is why aggressively learning about any area of interest reduces your fear to the point where you are ready to act and make changes. But if you're completely ignorant, if you have not read or learned anything about a subject, it will seem complicated and overwhelming. As a result, you'll be afraid to take the actions necessary to improve your life in that area.

The antidotes to fear and ignorance are desire and knowledge. The only real limitation on your abilities is the intensity of your desires. If you really want something badly enough, there are no limits on what you can achieve, and the more you learn about any subject, the more confident you become to make your goals a reality. As you increase your levels of desire and knowledge, you decrease the blockages of fear and ignorance and their companions: learned helplessness and the comfort zone. With desire and knowledge, you eventually replace fear and ignorance with courage and confidence.

The more you learn about anything that is important to you, the more courage you have to try and the more confident you are that you can eventually succeed. As Henry Ford once said, if you believe you can do a thing or you believe you cannot, in either case, you're probably right. The first breakthrough for me was discovering that I could learn anything I needed to learn to achieve any goal I could set for myself.

The second breakthrough was realizing that I was completely responsible for myself and everything that happened to me. No one was going to do it for me, and the only limits were the ones I set on myself by my own limited thinking.

My third breakthrough was learning that *all causation is mental*. Everything in your material world begins with a thought within your mental world. If you want to change something on the outside, you have to begin by changing it on the inside.

Four Powerful Mental Laws

1. The law of belief
2. The law of expectations
3. The law of attraction
4. The law of correspondence

There are four powerful mental laws that you need to know. It is essential to have these laws at your mental fingertips before we begin.

The first is the *law of belief*: whatever you believe with feeling becomes your reality. If you absolutely believe that you are destined to be a great success, nothing in the world can stop you from becoming that great success. If you absolutely believe that you are a good person with tremendous abilities and that you're going to do remarkable things with your life, that belief will express itself through all of your actions and will eventually become your reality. Your biggest job is to change your beliefs on the inside so that they are consistent with the realities you wish to enjoy on the outside.

The second law is the *law of expectations*: whatever you expect with confidence becomes your own self-fulfilling prophecy. If you expect to be successful, you eventually will be successful. If you expect to be happy and popular, you will be happy and popular. You are continually telling your own fortune by the way you talk about how things are going to turn out. Positive, successful, winning individuals have an attitude of positive self-expectancy. They expect to be successful in advance, and they're seldom disappointed.

The best way to predict the future is to create it, and you create your future by the way you approach everything that happens to you, either positively or negatively. If you approach each situation confidently expecting to learn or gain from it, you'll grow and progress and move towards your goals. You will also be a happier, more optimistic person that other people will want be around and help.

The third law is the *law of attraction*. This law says that you are a living magnet: you attract people and circumstances into your life that harmonize with your dominant thoughts, especially when they are emotionalized. We'll talk more about this later. But suffice it to say now, the more you think about something and the more excited you are about achieving it, the more you'll attract it into your life. Just as a magnet attracts iron filings, you'll attract the people, circumstances, ideas, opportunities, and resources necessary to achieve your goals. When you think big about yourself and your possibilities, you attract the forces necessary to turn them into reality.

The final law, which links them all, is the *law of correspondence*. This law says that your outer world reflects your inner world; wherever you go, there you are. Wherever you look, you see yourself.

Your outer world of wealth, work, relationships, and health will always reflect what is going on inside you.

These laws—belief, expectations, attraction, and correspondence—taken together are the keys to great accomplishments. When you begin to think big about your dreams and goals, you change your beliefs. You control your expectations; you activate the law of attraction. You bring about corresponding changes in the world around you.

Successful and happy people have a successful, happy mindset. Prosperous and wealthy people have a prosperous and wealthy mindset; kind, patient, gentle, loving people who enjoy wonderful relationships with their families and friends have kind, patient, loving mindsets. When you develop the same mindset that is in other successful people, you'll enjoy the same results and experiences that they do.

Becoming Unstoppable

The basic premise of this book is that by engaging in a series of proven mental exercises and applications, you can develop your mind and emotions to the point where you become unstoppable in achieving any goal you can set for yourself. You can develop yourself psychologically to the point where you become like an irresistible force of nature, like a flash flood, the tide coming in, or a powerful storm, sweeping everything before it. You can become so confident, courageous, strong, and resolute that you can set any goal for yourself with the firm knowledge that you can learn what you need to learn and do what you need to do to achieve it. You become so persistent and determined that nothing and no one can slow you down or alter your course, and you become truly unstoppable.

The starting point of becoming unstoppable in your mind and heart is for you to dream big dreams. Since everything you create in your outer world begins with a thought, the bigger dreams you dream, the bigger goals you'll achieve. All high-achieving men and women are dreamers. All peak performers are blue-sky thinkers: they continually allow their minds to float freely, and they look at the big, blue sky above them in terms of everything and anything that they could possibly be or have or do.

> Peak performers are blue-sky thinkers.

Average people have hopes, but leaders have vision. A vision is a mental picture of the future that you can see clearly before it appears in your reality. Leaders project several years into the future and see what it would look like. They take a mental journey five or ten years forward and imagine that they have achieved all of their goals. They then look back to the present, like looking from the top of a tall mountain down to the valley where they're standing in the present. Then they look at the path that they will have to take to get to where they want to be.

The most important part of great dreams and accomplishments is to define your ideal future vision: think about what you really want before thinking about what is possible for you. You dream big dreams by looking into the future and imagining that you have no limitations whatsoever on any of your abilities. When you imagine no limitations, you break the psychological chains of learned helplessness and the comfort zone. You rise above your current situation and pretend for a while that you have all the time, money, people, resources, education, knowledge, and experience that you could ever possibly want in order to be, have, or do anything that you could dream of.

Imagine your ideal lifestyle. Imagine your ideal job or income. Imagine where you would like to live and how you would like to spend each day, each week, each month. Imagine your ideal family life. Imagine your ideal state of health.

Here's an exercise for you. Take out a piece of paper, and at the top write the words "Dream List," underline it, and write down everything you can think of that you could ever possibly want if you had no limitations whatsoever.

The biggest obstacle to unlocking your potential and expanding your concept of your possibilities is your self-limiting beliefs, fears, and doubts. They hold you back more than anything else. If you're not careful, they can make you skeptical and even critical of yourself.

Psychologist Abraham Maslow once said that the biggest problem in modern society is men and women selling themselves short.

> The biggest problem in modern society is men and women selling themselves short.

What one great thing would you dare to dream if you knew you could not fail? If you were absolutely guaranteed of success in any one thing, big or small, long-term or short-term, what would it be? If a multibillionaire took a liking to you and offered to write you a check to cover any goal or goals that you could write down, what would you choose? If you could have any job, what would it be? If you could work for any kind of company, what kind of a company would it be? Where would it be, and what would it be doing? If your relationships could be perfect in every respect, what would they look like?

If money is your goal, remember that most of the people with money today started out without any at all. Everyone who is on the top today was once at the bottom. Everyone at the front of the line was once at the back of the line. Almost everyone who was wealthy was once poor. Most millionaires are self-made: they started out with nothing, and they worked their way up. Our world today even has self-made billionaires and multi-billionaires. These people started with little or nothing, and by thinking big, they unleash their own inner potential to accomplish extraordinary things.

Almost anything that anyone else has done you can do as well. So what are your goals? What are your dreams? Once you have a dream list, and you've written down everything you could possibly want to achieve if you had no limitations at all, if you were absolutely guaranteed of success, you can begin refining your list step by step to develop a blueprint for your life.

Henry David Thoreau once wrote, "Have you built your castles in the air? Good! That's where they should be built. Now go to work and build foundations under them." Once you've broken free from your limited thinking, like a balloon casting loose its lines and rising high into the sky, you can begin to turn your dreams and fantasies into concrete, practical goals and specific plans of action.

Your ability to set goals and make plans for their accomplishment is the master skill of success. With it, there are no limits on what you can do, and this is the next stage of the process.

> ### Seven Steps to Goal Setting
> 1. Decide exactly what you want.
> 2. Write your goals down on paper.
> 3. Determine the price you will have to pay.
> 4. Make a plan in writing.
> 5. Take action.
> 6. Do something every day that moves you toward your goal.
> 7. Decide that you will never quit.

Seven Steps to Goal Setting

There are seven steps to goal setting that you can use over and over in any situation to accomplish any objective you could ever want. In combination, these seven steps represent a powerful formula that will change your life almost immediately after you begin using it.

Step one is to *decide exactly what you want*. A real goal is clear, specific, measurable, and time-bounded. A nongoal, a wish, or a fantasy just floats in the air. People with clear, specific goals, who know exactly what they want, are very different from people who are going through life hoping for the best. Your ability to decide exactly what you want out of your wishes and fantasies is one of your most important responsibilities.

> Your ability to decide exactly what you want is one of your most important responsibilities.

People often come up to me at my seminars and ask me what their goals should be. I tell them that only they can decide. It's amazing how many of them tell me how hard it is to set goals, and I agree with them. It is hard, but it's essential. With clear goals, you can do almost anything; without them, you can do virtually nothing.

People often fail in life because they waste so much of their time doing things of low value or no value, and they waste so much time because they have no real idea of what represents value to them.

Here's a simple question to help you decide whether or not you should do anything: does it move you toward one of your goals or not? If it helps you to achieve a goal that you have set for yourself, it's a good use of time. If it doesn't, it's a poor use of time. If you get into the habit of only doing the things that represent good uses of time, soon you'll find that every hour of every day is taken up by doing things that are helping you in some way. You'll have no time left to devote to things that don't do you any good.

Many people waste so much time on things like watching television or Internet surfing because they have no clear way to determine what a good use of time is. But when they start to set very clear goals, knowing exactly what they want, they become increasingly impatient with activities that are not helping them. They watch less and less television; they waste less time on social media. They read the news quickly, if at all. They become far more selective with their friends and social activities and only spend time with people from whom they can learn and benefit. But as the old saying goes, if you don't know where you're going, any road will take you there.

Step two is to *write your goals down on paper*. When you take up a pad of paper and a pen and write down your goals, something quite incredible happens between the brain and the hand: you activate the laws of expectation, attraction, and correspondence simultaneously. You intensify your belief and deepen your conviction that your goal is possible for you. The very act of writing down your goals gives you a sense of control and personal power that increases your determination to do whatever is necessary to achieve them. And the speed at which your goals begin to materialize after you've written them down is nothing short of miraculous. Thousands of my graduates have come back and told me about the amazing things that have happened in their lives immediately after they began writing down what they wanted.

Step three is to *determine the price you're going to have to pay to achieve your goal*. Make a list of everything that you're going to have to do if you want to make your goal a reality. Will you have to start a little earlier, work a little harder, and stay a little later? Write it down. Will you have to upgrade your knowledge and skills and take additional courses? Again, write it down. Will you have to change jobs, industries, or careers in order to do everything that you are meant to do? Write it down as well.

The law of cause and effect is the iron law of the universe. For everything that you want, there's a price that must be paid, and it must be paid in full and in advance.

The law of sowing and reaping is *not* the law of reaping and sowing: you have to put in before you get out. You have to give before you receive. You have to pay the price before you enjoy the reward. Your willingness to do whatever you need to do, pay whatever price, go whatever distance, make whatever sacrifice is the true measure of how badly you want your goal.

Many people sabotage their own success by deciding that they're willing to pay a high price for a particular goal but are not quite willing to pay the full price. This is like wanting to win in a poker game but not being willing to match the final bet made by the other player. You end up losing the whole hand.

> The ability to develop written goals and plans is the master skill of success.

Step four in this process is to *make a plan*, also in writing. The ability to develop written goals and plans is the master skill of success. A plan is a list of all the things that you can think of that you're going to have to do to achieve your goal. Once you've made your list—which you can add to as you gain more information and experience—you organize it in terms of priority and sequence.

What are the most important things on the list that you'll have to do to achieve your goal? What things will you have to do first, and what things will you have to do second? Which items depend on completing other items first? A plan of action gives you a track to run on. It increases your level of belief and intensifies your desire for the goal. It activates the law of attraction even more. You begin to become convinced that your goal is possible and achievable. You become excited, and you begin to see things around you that you could do and possibilities that you might not have been aware of in the absence of a written plan.

Step five is to *take action* of some kind in the direction of your goal. Once you've set a goal, written it down, determined the price that you're going to have to pay, and made a plan, you must take some action immediately, even if it's only making a phone call or doing one small thing. The Bible says that faith without works is dead. There's something powerful in willingness to take a specific action in faith in the direction of your goal, even though it may have no guarantee of success. Your action itself seems to trigger all kinds of other powers and forces in the universe. When you act, you demonstrate to yourself and others that you are serious about your goal. Until you have taken a specific, irrevocable action in the direction you've decided to go, you have merely engaged in an interesting exercise. You have loaded the gun, but you have not fired it. You have put your key into the ignition, but you haven't turned it on.

Step six is to *do something every day that moves you toward a goal that is important to you*. This is an incredibly important principle that I will go into at greater length later, but to maintain a high level of courage, confidence, and self-motivation, you must be doing something every single day that gives you a feeling of forward motion and progress. Your job is to build yourself up to the point where you genuinely feel unstoppable, and the only way that you can do this is by refusing to stop, by keeping on keeping on.

Finally, step number seven is *to decide in advance that you will never quit*. Once you've set off towards your goal, no matter how many setbacks or obstacles you experience, you will keep on picking yourself up and persisting until you eventually succeed by deciding in advance that you will persist. No matter what the difficulty, when the difficulties do arise—as they certainly will—you will be psychologically prepared to plow through them without hesitation. This principle of persistence is vital to great accomplishments.

> Persistence is vital to great accomplishments.

As I said at the outset of this book, we are living in a wonderful world, surrounded by more opportunities and possibilities to achieve our dreams than have existed in all of human history. As we've seen, learned helplessness and the comfort zone are the two major mental obstacles to dreaming great dreams and setting great goals.

You overcome fear and ignorance with desire and knowledge. And the two qualities that flow out of intense desire and expanded knowledge are the courage and confidence necessary to achieve anything you want. You translate your dreams into concrete realities by turning them into goals. You decide exactly what you want. You write it down. You set a deadline, and you determine the price you're going to have to pay to achieve it. You make written plans of action to achieve your goals, and you do something every day to move forward, resolving in advance to never, never give up.

Vision and Leadership

In more than 3,300 studies of leadership, the one common denominator of all leaders was found to be *vision*. Leaders have the ability to visualize, and this is the power source that you put behind your goals. Whatever you can clearly see on the inside, you'll eventually experience on the outside. Visualize your goals with as much clarity and vividness as possible. Visualize them intensely, and create within yourself the same feeling that you would have if you had already achieved them. Visualize your goals frequently, and replay a picture of your goal as already realized on the screen of your mind as many times a day as you possibly can. Finally, visualize your goals for as long as you possibly can, preferably just before falling asleep each night.

Repeat these exercises of visualization with vividness, intensity, frequency, and duration, until your goals become absolutely clear, living, breathing, exciting pictures in your mind. The more skilled you become at moving from the dream through the goal to the visualization, the more motivated you will be, the more courage and confidence you will have, and the more unstoppable you will become.

Success is an inside job. It's a state of mind. It begins within you and is soon reflected in the world around you. By dreaming big dreams, you become a leader. By writing down your goals and making plans to accomplish them, you take full control of your life.

Key Points in This Chapter

1. Two major obstacles to success are learned helplessness and the comfort zone.
2. Learning will reduce fear and enable you to act.
3. Four powerful mental laws—belief, expectations, attraction, and correspondence—will lead you to great achievements.
4. You can become unstoppable in any goal you set for yourself.
5. You dream big dreams by looking into the future and imagining that you have no limitations whatsoever.

6. The biggest obstacle to success is self-limiting beliefs, fears, and doubts.
7. Use the seven steps to goal setting.
8. Visualize your goals as clearly as you can. See them as already accomplished.

two

Commit to Excellence

As we've seen in the previous chapter, the starting point of extraordinary achievements is to break loose from the mental bonds that hold you back. Dreaming great dreams and setting great goals is the starting point of thinking, seeing, and feeling yourself as capable of achieving far more than you've ever done before.

The next step is to *commit to excellence*: to decide right now to be the best at what you do. It used to be that you needed to be excellent to rise to the top of your field or market. Today excellence is taken for granted: you have to be excellent just to get into the market in the first place. Then you have to constantly improve, getting better and better week by week and month by month, if you want to keep up with the competition.

The market only pays superior rewards for superior performance. It pays average rewards for average performance, and below average rewards—unemployment and bankruptcy—for below average performance. The race is on, and your competitors are more capable and determined than they've ever been before. They'll be even more capable and determined next year, the year after, and for the rest of your career. In every field, the top 20 percent of companies make 80 percent of the profits. The top 20 percent of salespeople make 80 percent of the sales and 80 percent of the income. The top 20 percent enjoy the great rewards of money, pride, satisfaction, and reputation that go along with being the best in their fields.

> The most important quality of high-achieving men and women is ambition.

Perhaps the most important quality of high-achieving men and women is *ambition*. Every day they see themselves, think about themselves, and conduct themselves as though they were among the elite in their fields.

They set high goals for themselves, and they continually work to exceed those goals. For them, quotas are minimums, not maximums. They look upon the accomplishments of everyone else as challenges to be even better—and so must you.

Self-Esteem: The Core of Your Personality

The core of your personality is your level of self-esteem. This is best defined as how much you like yourself, respect yourself, value yourself, and think of yourself as an important and worthwhile person. Your level of self-esteem is the root source of your energy, enthusiasm, motivation, inspiration, and drive. The more you like and respect yourself, the better you will do at everything you attempt, and the better you do, the more you will like and respect yourself. These factors reinforce each other continually.

Self-esteem and self-efficacy, or how well you perform, are flip sides of the same coin. You can only genuinely like and respect yourself when you know deep in your heart that you are really good at what you do. A sense of personal mastery is absolutely essential to the healthy human personality. Every single thing that you do in an excellent fashion boosts your self-esteem and makes you feel better about yourself and feel more confident of performing at even higher levels in the future.

Great achievements require high levels of courage and confidence and a continual willingness to move out of your comfort zone, to break the bonds of learned helplessness that hold most people back. The higher your self-esteem, the more powerful, positive, and determined you are and the more willing you are to take chances to step out in faith and hang in there longer than anyone else.

The better you become in your chosen field, the stronger and better you become in other areas of your life as well. In fact, it's impossible for you to be happy or successful for very long unless you know in your heart that you are very good at what you do.

Resolve right now to overcome any obstacle, pay any price, or go any distance to achieve this level of excellence. Set a goal to be among the top 10 percent of performers in your field, and then do whatever it takes to get there.

Fortunately, getting to the top of your field is easier than you think. The great majority of people never even think about personal excellence. Most of the people around you are content to do their jobs for better or for worse, then to go to the bar or go home and watch television. But when you begin to make those extra efforts that enable you to excel, you'll find that, like a runner going into a sprint, you soon move ahead of the pack of ordinary runners.

Critical Success Factors

One of the most important ideas that has emerged in recent decades is the *winning edge concept*. This concept has been proven over and over. It says that small differences in ability can lead to enormous differences in results. Research shows that the top people in every field are only a little bit better in the critical things that they do, but being a little bit better consistently soon adds up to an enormous difference in results. In fact, all you have to do is be about 3 percent better in each of the key things that you do in your job and then maintain and increase this gap as you continue to evolve and grow through learning and practice in order to eventually emerge in the top 10 or even 5 percent of people in your business.

This brings us to another key concept: *critical success factors*, or CSFs. Critical success factors are the things that you absolutely, positively have to do well to be successful in your job, whatever it is. They are called critical success factors because a weakness in any one of them is critical: it will hold you back from using all the others. Your weakest critical success factor sets the height at which you will perform in all your other skill areas.

In regard to physical health, there are three such factors: proper diet, proper exercise, and proper rest. Almost all health problems will result from a weakness in one of those three areas.

In most professional fields, there are usually five to seven critical success factors. In selling, they are (1) prospecting, (2) getting appointments, (3) establishing trust and rapport, (4) identifying the customer's problem, (5) presenting your product or service as the ideal solution to the problem, (6) getting an agreement to proceed, and (7) personal management skills. If you excel at all seven of these, you will be at the top of your field in no time.

In management, the critical success factors are usually (1) planning, (2) organizing, (3) selecting the right people, (4) delegating, (5) supervising, (6) innovating, and (7) communicating both upwards and downwards. If you're excellent at every one of those except, for example, delegating, that one weakness alone will hold you back in your career as a manager.

> Excellence starts with identifying your critical success factors.

You start to excel in your field by first identifying your critical success factors. Define them clearly and write them down. Then give yourself a score of 1 to 10 in each, with 1 being the lowest and 10 being the highest. Wherever you are scoring 7 or below, you know that you have work to do to bring it up. Your job is to bring up your weakest critical success factor as quickly as possible, and then to develop a plan to bring them all up gradually over time. Every step you take toward improving yourself in your critical success factors will make you better and better at your job. The better you get, the more you'll like and respect yourself, the better you'll feel, the more energy and enthusiasm you'll have, and the more unstoppable you'll become.

Personal Strategic Planning

It used to be that corporations did strategic planning on a regular basis, and individuals were encouraged to set personal goals. Today, however, all that has changed. Today you must regularly engage in personal strategic planning. Here you look upon yourself as an organization, and you make more detailed long-range plans for your activities and goals in every part of your life.

It's no longer enough to write down some goals, make some plans, and get busy. Today you have to spend far more time thinking into the future, analyzing and planning the steps that you need to take to make your future dreams into present realities. Then you have to manage yourself better than ever before.

Sometimes I ask my audiences, how many people here are self-employed? Usually about 10 to 15 percent of the audience will raise their hands. I then stop the seminar and ask them again, how many people here are really self-employed? Then I wait. It doesn't take very long. People look at one another and then back at me and then back at one another again. Soon one hand after another begins to go up. Eventually, almost the whole room has their hands up. After a little thought, almost everyone realizes that they are all self-employed.

The biggest mistake that you can make is to think that you ever work for anyone else but yourself. The fact is that you are always self-employed from the time you take your first job until the time you retire. No matter who signs your paycheck, you are working for yourself. You are the president of an entrepreneurial personal services company with one employee: yourself.

In the long run, as a result of the things that you do or fail to do, you determine how much you get paid. If you want an increase in pay, you can go to the nearest mirror and negotiate with your boss.

Sometimes people argue with me about this. They say that the pay schedules in their business and industry are determined by factors over which they have no control. But then I point out to them that it was they who decided to go to work in that business or industry, and it is they who decide to stay there. If you're not happy with any part of your work, it's up to you to change it.

Benjamin Disraeli, prime minister of Great Britain in the nineteenth century, once said, "Never complain, never explain." If there's a part of your work life that you don't like, don't waste your time complaining about it; instead, take action. As Shakespeare wrote, "Take arms against a sea of troubles, and by opposing, end them."

Seeing yourself as the president of your own personal services corporation requires accepting total responsibility for everything you are and everything you ever will be. This is an enormous thought for most people. It's both scary and exhilarating. You are where you are and what you are because you have decided to be there. Everything you accomplish for the rest of your life will be solely determined by the actions that you take or fail to take. You are responsible. You are in charge. You are in control. You are your own boss, and there are no limits on you except those that you allow the outside world to place on yourself and your thinking.

> You are responsible. You are in charge. You are in control.

When you begin thinking of yourself as a personal services corporation, you will begin thinking in terms of personal strategic planning. The parallels between corporate planning and personal planning are very similar. The purpose of strategic planning for a corporation is to achieve the highest return on equity invested in the business. Strategic plans and tactics are aimed at reorganizing the company's resources and activities so that it achieves a higher rate of financial return on its resources than it was achieving before.

To put it another way, strategic planning is aimed at increasing the ratio of outputs to inputs. The management practices popular today, such as restructuring, reorganizing, reengineering, and reinventing, are aimed at increasing outputs and rates of return on equity. Return on equity is often abbreviated as ROE. Your personal ROE, however, refers to return on *energy*. Personal strategic planning involves organizing your life and restructuring your activities to increase the satisfaction and rewards you get from the investment of your life in your work.

Let us say, for example, that you've decided to double your income in the next three to five years. This is a reasonable goal, and many people around you are successfully working toward it every day. But if you want to double your income, you have to double the value of your output relative to your input. It's no miracle. Success is not an accident. Profits do not fall from heaven. Financial results come from producing valuable goods and services that the market is willing to pay for. If you want to increase the amount you get out, you have to plan to increase the amount that you put in.

The critical factor that determines the success or failure of any company is its competitive advantage or area of excellence. Every company comes into being because it has a unique capacity to offer the market something better than its competitors.

The competitive advantage, or *unique selling proposition*, of a company determines its rate of growth, its level of sales, its height of profitability, and its very survival. Companies without a competitive advantage soon disappear from the marketplace, to be replaced by other companies with clear, unmistakable competitive advantages that customers can and will pay for.

You are no different. As a president of a company of one, you too must develop and maintain meaningful competitive advantage. You must develop an area of uniqueness. To rise to the top of your field, you must excel in your work. Your choices and decisions about your competitive advantage will be the critical determinants of your financial success.

Here's an exercise for you. Complete this sentence: "If I could do X really well, I could make all the money I wanted." Your job is to fill in the blank.

What one skill, if you had it and did it in an excellent fashion over and over, would have the greatest positive impact on your income? If you could wave a magic wand and be outstanding in any one part of your work, which part would you choose? This is the critical success factor that you need to go to work on right away.

Zero-Based Thinking

There are several concepts in personal strategic planning that can lead to act more effectively and change your life. The first is *zero-based thinking*. Draw a line under all your activities. Imagine that you are starting over. Ask yourself this question: "Is there anything in my life that, knowing what I now know, I wouldn't get into again if I had to do it over?"

This is one of the most important single questions you will ever learn. You can apply it to every part of your life. One critical problem in personal strategic planning is attempting to make something work when you wouldn't have gotten into it the first place if you had to do it over again. Often when I consult with companies, they ask me how they can turn around the falling sales of a particular product or service. I ask them, knowing what you now know, would you introduce this product or service to the marketplace? They almost invariably assure me that knowing what they now know, they would never have brought the product out in the first place. My advice to them then is always the same: kill it. If there's anything in your life or your work that you wouldn't get into today, knowing what you now know, it is an excellent candidate for creative abandonment.

Your most valuable asset is your time. Every aspect of your life merely represents your ability to trade your time for results, and your time is limited. If you use it ineffectively, you no longer have that same quantity of time available for getting good results somewhere else. You must be extremely jealous of your time usage. You must be adamant about not spending your time on activities of low value. If you want to get the highest return on your energy, you must downsize, outsource, and eliminate all activities that do not represent the highest and best use of your time.

Be extremely jealous of your time usage.

A key strategic planning concept is the 80/20 rule: 80 percent of your results will come from 20 percent of your activities. But the 20 percent of activities that account for most of the value are invariably the most difficult and challenging ones. The 80 percent of activities that only account for 20 percent of your results are usually fun and easy.

Being human, you have a natural tendency to do things that are easier, even though they're not particularly valuable or important. You must fight this tendency with all your strength. Focus your energies on the one or two things that will really make a difference.

Competitive Advantage

Your first question for yourself is, what is my competitive advantage? What are you absolutely excellent at doing? What do you do as well or better than almost anyone else in your business? What unique set of skills do you have that account for most of your success to date? Where are you really good?

Your second question is, looking objectively at the trends in my industry, to ask, what will my competitive advantage be in three to five years? If you can project yourself three to five years into the future, what will you be doing in an excellent fashion at that time?

Many people have trouble answering either of these questions. They are not sure what their competitive advantage is today, and as a result they have no idea of what it will be in the future. If you are in this situation, you are in great danger of underachieving and even failing in your career.

So here's the next question: what should your competitive advantage be? If you could be absolutely outstanding in any one area, what should it be? If you're not sure, ask your boss or your coworkers. Ask them, if I was really, really good in any one area, what one skill would have the greatest positive impact on my results? The people around you, especially your boss, can usually tell you quite quickly the answer to this question.

Once you have the answer, that becomes your new goal or target.

You think big about that area, and you imagine that you have the capacity to be absolutely outstanding in that activity. You then set it as a goal, write it down, set a deadline, make a plan, and go to work on yourself. In no time at all, you'll begin to develop the winning edges in that area and start to move ahead of the crowd.

> ### Four Strategic Marketing Valuables
> 1. Specialization
> 2. Differentiation
> 3. Segmentation
> 4. Concentration

Four Strategic Variables

There are four strategic variables for marketing yourself and your services. Your effectiveness in each of these areas will determine your income and your future. They are: (1) specialization, (2) differentiation, (3) segmentation, and (4) concentration.

SPECIALIZATION

Specialization means deciding exactly what you're going to do and do well. All really successful people are specialized. They have a reputation for being very good in a particular area. They don't try to be all things to all men or a jack-of-all-trades.

A successful business will specialize in a particular type of customer. It'll often specialize in a particular product or service for a particular type of customer. A successful salesperson will specialize in selling a particular product or service to a particular type of customer. A successful salesperson will *not* try to sell everything to everyone, but will instead sell very specific things to very specific people.

What is your area of specialization? What will it be in the future? What should it be if you want to move to the top of your field? What could it be if you were to stand back and dream even bigger dreams and set even higher goals for yourself?

DIFFERENTIATION

The second strategic variable is *differentiation*. This is the most important single part of all sales, marketing, and business development. This is the key to success in your career.

Differentiation is defined as the way that you separate yourself from everyone else in your field who is offering something similar. Your area of differentiation is your area of excellence, your competitive advantage, your area of uniqueness, or your unique selling proposition. Imagine that a prospective customer were to ask you, what about your product or service is different, better, and superior to any other similar product or service offered by any other company in today's market? How would you answer? If you had to explain honestly to a critical prospect how and why your product or service is superior to that of your competitors, what would you say?

Most salespeople don't know the answer to this question. Even many business owners are vague about the answer, but you must be absolutely crystal clear about it if you want to make more sales in an increasingly competitive market.

As an individual doing personal strategic planning, you must ask this question of yourself: what unique skills do you have that make you superior to anyone else offering to do the same job that you are doing? What skills would it be useful for you to have? If you're not currently outstanding in your field, what steps do you need to take, beginning immediately, to get yourself to the point where you stand out from all the rest?

Certain companies are going through an exercise that is very disturbing to their employees. They're calling everyone in and firing the entire staff. After everyone is fired, they announce that they're going to be outsourcing every single job and that each person can reapply for their job as though they were outside contractors presenting a proposal. Proposals for their jobs should include a description of what they intended to do, how they intended to do it, how much they would charge for it, and how the company could justify paying them the amounts they want for it. Finally, the company tells the employees that they will be competing against other people who will be submitting proposals for the same jobs.

As you can imagine, most employees fall apart when they're presented with this exercise. It is almost overwhelming for them to think through their work and describe it in the form of a proposal along with a justification for why they should be paid the amount they're asking.

If you were put into this position and you had to write out a proposal for your job, starting with the most important and valuable things you do, how would you present yourself? How would you sell yourself to your current employer? How would you sell yourself to your current customers? Above all, what are your core competencies? What special talents and abilities do you have that make you valuable and set you apart from others? If you're not sure about your core competencies, what should they be or could they be? These answers will determine your future.

SEGMENTATION

The third strategic area is *segmentation*: dividing your markets into segments based on identifying those customers who can most benefit from your area of specialization and your particular area of excellence within that area. With segmentation, you identify your ideal customers. Who are they? Where are they? What do they have in common? What are their ages, incomes, education levels, backgrounds, positions, and experiences?

Today, marketing is focused on niches and microniches. Sales and marketing are increasingly personal and individual, focused on prospective customers with special qualities and characteristics. Who are your customers?

CONCENTRATION

The final part of strategy, perhaps the most important of all, is *concentration*. This is your ability to combine your energies and resources and focus them on those customers or market opportunities where you have the greatest chance of success in the shortest period of time. Your ability to concentrate single-mindedly on your highest value opportunities will do more to increase your return on energy than any other factor.

> Businesses fail because of low sales. Businesses succeed because of high sales. Everything else is commentary.

Dun & Bradstreet is one of the world's leading suppliers of business information, with a database covering 240 million companies. At one point, they put their research on failed businesses into a computer and they came up with a single conclusion: businesses fail because of low sales; businesses succeed because of high sales; everything else is commentary.

Finding Your Area of Excellence

As the president of your own company engaged in personal strategic planning, your job is to ensure the highest possible level of sales of your personal services. This means that you must specialize, differentiate, segment, and concentrate. You must become excellent at doing one or two things that the market will pay for; then you must continually get better and better in those areas.

Do you know how you can tell when you are really good at what you do? It's simple: people will continually try to hire you away from your current employment. You will get regular job offers. If you are self-employed, you'll have more business than you can handle. You'll get a steady flow of recommendations and referrals from satisfied customers. You'll have complete job security. You'll know that if something happened to your current job, you could walk across the street and get another job tomorrow. You never worry about the ups or downs in the economy, because you're always dealing with far more opportunities than you can handle in a twenty-four-hour day.

When you're one of the best in your field, you feel terrific about yourself and you have complete control over your future.

You may be wondering how you determine your area of excellence if you don't already have one. If you are already very good at what you do, you have to know that with change taking place so rapidly, you will find yourself in another field, doing a different job with a different area of excellence within a few years.

> Successful people do what they love to do.

This brings us to one of the most important parts of any part of life: successful people do what they love to do. They do what they do for the art and joy of it. They would do what they do even if they weren't getting paid for it. A good question to continually ask yourself is, what would I choose to work at if I won $1 million cash tomorrow?

If most people won $1 million, they would immediately quit their current jobs. If you would do that, you are in great danger of wasting your career and your life. Self-made millionaires almost invariably say that their secret to success was finding out what they enjoyed doing and then doing it with their whole heart. Most successful people feel that they don't really work at all. Some of them say, "I haven't worked a day in my life." Their work and their play are intermingled: they don't know where one begins and the other ends. When they're not at work, they think about it and talk about it, and when they are at work, they lose themselves in it.

Selecting Your Ideal Job

According to labor statistics, there are easily 100,000 different jobs that you could be doing, and most of the jobs that people will be doing in two decades haven't even been invented yet. Of the many thousands of jobs that exist, there are a variety of jobs at which you could work and earn a reasonable living. Your goal must be to select the ideal job for you—the one that gives you the greatest joy, satisfaction, and rewards—and channel all of your energies into becoming excellent in that area. How do you do this?

You are extraordinary. You are born with unique talents and abilities that make you completely different from all other human beings that have ever existed. There is no one who has the unique and remarkable combination of experiences, ideas, thoughts, feelings, education, and imagination that you do. You have within you right now the ability to be, have, or do, virtually anything you can imagine. The key to success is to identify your natural abilities and to develop these talents. It is almost as though you are engineered in a specific way, and if you can find the area for which you were specifically engineered, you can achieve more in a few years than most people achieve in a lifetime.

> You have within you right now the ability to be, have, or do, virtually anything you can imagine.

The starting point of identifying your unique areas of ability is to look back over your life. Which activities have given you your greatest results and rewards? When you were in school, what subjects interested you the most? What subjects did you get the best grades in? You'll always be best at doing something that holds your attention, that captures your interest, that naturally attracts you. One test for whether or not something is right for you is your desire to learn more about it. Whatever your area of natural talent, you'll enjoy reading about it, talking about it, and learning about it. In addition, you'll naturally admire the people who are the most successful in this field.

Do What You Love

One test that has emerged from the research is simple. Look back to what you most enjoyed doing when you were between the ages of seven and fourteen years. At this time, you were completely free to bury yourself in any subject that attracted you, so what did you most enjoy doing? If you don't remember, ask one of your parents. They will usually remember how you spent your time when you were younger.

Dale Carnegie once wrote, "Tell me what gives a person his greatest feeling of importance, and I will tell you his entire philosophy of life." What gives you your greatest feeling of importance? What gives you a heightened feeling of self-esteem when you do it successfully? What do you most enjoy doing, so much so that you are drawn back to it continuously?

Napoleon Hill, author of *Think and Grow Rich*, said that one of the great secrets of success is to decide what you most enjoy doing and then find a way to earn a good living at it. Most people get it backward: they do what they feel they have to do so that they can earn the time and money necessary to do what they really want to do. Your goal should be to reverse this order: do what you really enjoy doing so that you can get better and better at doing more and more of what you most enjoy.

In this process, one of the most important qualities that you'll require is courage. You need courage to face the fact that right now you might not be doing what you were meant to do. Most people back into their jobs and their careers like backing a car into the garage. They take the job that is offered to them at the time they're starting work or making the transition from one job to another. They do what is assigned to them to do. Their entire lives are geared around the expectations of the people who sign their paychecks. If they're not careful, years will go by and they'll completely lose sight of the child in them who started off in life with a world of untapped possibilities and potentialities lying ahead.

Joseph Campbell, the late professor of mythology, told a story about something that took place in a small local restaurant that he patronized with his wife. One day, another couple, along with their eight-year-old son, came in and sat down for dinner. Halfway through the dinner, the boy said that he didn't like his dinner and he wasn't going to eat it. The father became extremely angry and insisted that he eat it whether he liked it or not. The boy refused and said to his father, "But I don't want to eat it." At this, the father blew up and shouted, "You don't want to! What does that have to do with anything? I never did anything I wanted to do in my whole life."

Campbell pointed out that many people are in that same situation. They feel that they have lived their whole lives doing things that other people wanted them to do because they never had the courage just to do what they wanted. Campbell then said that the key to success and happiness in life was to follow your bliss—to do what you most love to do. Sit down, look over the landscape of your life, and decide what things you have enjoyed doing more than anything else—the things that you would do if you had no limitations—and then do only those.

Many of the most successful men and women have at one point gotten up and walked away from a situation that they realized was not consistent with what they most enjoyed. They decided that they were going to do what they loved to do, not what they felt they had to do. They looked deep within themselves, assessed their own natural talents and abilities, and often changed their whole careers.

Once when I was considering changing careers, I had a very good idea of what I wanted to do. I asked a friend of mine what he thought I might be good at doing. He replied without a moment's hesitation, "You would be excellent at teaching and giving seminars." Although that was exactly what I had been thinking, I wasn't sure about changing my whole career into a completely unknown field. My friend's comment made me realize that often the people around you can clearly see what you should be doing even if you can't see it yourself.

You might ask the people who know you well what they think your ideal line of work would be.

The people who know you and care about you will often give you remarkable ideas and insights that will reveal your heart's desire: the one special thing that you were put on this earth to do. No one else can do it the same way that you can. It may have been calling to you for many years, like the sound of distant music. It has attracted you since you were young. Perhaps you've never told anyone about it. Perhaps deep in your heart, you were afraid of the enormous changes you would have to make to pursue your heart's desire, but you will never truly be happy or satisfied until you let yourself go and throw your whole heart into this desire.

You are not what you are; you are what you can be.

In his book *Discover the Power within You*, Eric Butterworth wrote that you are not what you are; you are what you can be. You are not what you are, but you are what you may be when you discover and develop your talents and abilities to the full. One mark of personal leadership is that you see yourself as you really are. You are completely honest. You acknowledge that you are completely responsible, the president of your own personal services corporation. You accept that excellent rewards only come from excellent performance. You view yourself strategically, and you plan every part of your life—including your own personal training and development program—to ensure that you become one of the best in your field. You leave nothing to chance. You don't hope for miracles or wish for a lucky break. You recognize that if it's to be, it's up to you.

Since you know you're going to have to spend the rest of your life working at something, you decide in advance that you will do what you love to do. You will become everything you are capable of becoming by following your unique talents and abilities, wherever they lead. You will only work at something you enjoy with people you enjoy doing work that makes a difference in the world. You set high standards for yourself. You think big about your career and your future. You recognize that anything that anyone else has done, you can probably do as well. Once you've decided what it is, you throw your whole heart into doing it in an excellent fashion.

Key Points in This Chapter

1. Decide right now to be the best at what you do.
2. Your self-esteem is the root source of your energy and inspiration.
3. The *winning edge concept* says that small differences in ability can lead to enormous differences in results.
4. *Critical success factors* are the things that you have to do well to be successful.
5. Use personal strategic planning. Look at yourself as an organization.
6. Everyone is self-employed.
7. One critical success factor is the *competitive advantage.*
8. Ask yourself: "Is there anything in my life that, knowing what I now know, I wouldn't get into again if I had to do it over?" If there is, get out of it as fast as possible.
9. The secret to success is finding out what you enjoy doing and then doing it with your whole heart.

three

Harness Your Unlimited Thinking Power

You are a potential genius. Your amazing brain has more than 171 billion cells, each connected to as many as 20,000 other cells and together making up so many combinations that their number is reckoned to surpass that of all the molecules in the known universe. You have the capacity to learn at incredible rates and retain more information than you can imagine. It is said that when an educated person dies, the equivalent of a library burns down. This library is contained between your ears.

Knowledge Is Capital

Throughout human history, value has always been contained in land, labor, capital, furniture, fixtures, machinery, and other hard assets. The primary creators of value were the people who could combine these various resources together to produce products and services for the marketplace. Over recent decades, we have seen change take place at a speed that is virtually unimaginable. In

1950, 15 percent of the American population lived on the farm, raising food for the other 85 percent who lived in the cities. Today, 2 percent of the population lives on farms, and they produce enough food not only for America, but huge surpluses that are exported or even given away to the entire world.

Over the past two centuries, we've moved from the agricultural age to the industrial age to the service age to the information age. The primary source of value today is not land, labor, and capital, but knowledge, information, and ideas. This means that the greatest wealth you could possess is between your ears. You can have an unlimited future merely by tapping into your brainpower and harnessing it like a powerful engine to take you anywhere or to get you anything you want. In May 2024, Apple had a market capitalization of $2.91 *trillion*. That value is almost entirely based on knowledge and information.

If you own a company, your chief assets go home every single day. At five o'clock they walk out the door; your entire building could burn to the ground, but as long as your people got out of the fire, you could walk across the street and start your business again. The chief assets of any organization, and any individual, are brainpower, not brute power. They are in mental strength rather than in physical strength.

> The chief assets of any organization, and any individual, are brainpower.

In generations past, it may have taken many years for a person to build up enough capital to start and build a successful business in manufacturing or services. Today, such a business can be a liability. A change in technology on the other side of the world can render a $100 million manufacturing plant obsolete in a few months.

What you have between your ears is your chief asset. It can be invaluable. It is completely portable; it is malleable and can be shaped and increased almost without limits if you know how. An immigrant could arrive at any major airport in America with the ability to build a billion-dollar computer industry in his head. He could walk up to customs, open his hands, and walk through saying, "Nothing to declare." His assets are all in his head.

Today the primary source of value is knowledge. Since you can get all the knowledge you want from countless sources, the amount of value that you can accumulate and create is unlimited as well. No matter what your background, you can start from wherever you are and increase your mental assets, your performance, and your income.

The wonderful thing about knowledge is that it can be reproduced hundreds of thousands, even millions of times, without losing its value. It is the one commodity that can be virtually infinite in application. If you come up with a new idea on how to do something faster or better, that idea can be spread around the world in no time at all and be in the hands of millions of people who can also use it to improve their lives and their work, and it will still have its original value to you.

In the last chapter, we talked about the winning edge concept and critical success factors. With regard to brainpower, these mean that very small differences in the way you think can lead to tremendous differences in performance. You don't need to go back to the university and get years of education to bring your knowledge up to the level where it can pay off for you. Sometimes very small changes in what you're doing right now, right where you are, can bring about amazing results.

If a horse runs in a race and wins by a nose, it earns ten times the prize money of a horse that comes in second by a nose. Does this mean that the horse that comes in first is ten times faster, twice as fast, or even 10 percent faster? No. The horse that wins is only a nose faster. By the same token, your possession of one small piece of information at the right time and in the right place can enable you to make an extraordinary difference.

The most successful people today are those who are continually investing in learning and growing their intellectual asset base. They have an adaptive mentality: they're continually open to new information and new approaches. The biggest mistake that many people make—especially those who graduate from a university—is believing that everything they know about a subject at the moment is all they need to know. They fall into the intelligence trap of the unconscious incompetent: the person who does not know and does not know that he does not know. This is the truly hopeless case. The beginning of all wisdom is the awareness of how ignorant you really are.

> The beginning of all wisdom is the awareness of how ignorant you are.

I've traveled in many countries and met many highly intelligent and successful people. I've worked with many millionaires, multimillionaires, and even billionaires. I've worked at the highest level of government with some of the smartest men and women who have ever lived. The one thing that they all have in common is that they never become impressed by their own intelligence. In fact, the smarter they get, the humbler they become, and the less they look upon themselves as experts in any way.

The artist and inventor Leonardo da Vinci (1459–1519) earned the epithet "universal man" because he was supposed to have been current with all the sciences of the day, knowing everything there was to know about everything. But at that time, 500 years ago, the amount of knowledge available was limited. The number of books available was limited. The number of scientists, philosophers, and researchers were limited as well. Today, it's impossible for one person to know everything about even one small subject. Just look at modern medicine. Great minds spend their entire lives studying the workings of the inner ear or the trachea or one of the organs of the body, and even though they spend their whole lives specializing in a particular part of the body, they never learn everything there is to know about even that one organ.

Sometimes I ask my audiences if there's anyone here who's a know-it-all. Of course no one raises their hand. Then I explain what a know-it-all really is: a person who feels that they know everything they need to know about their subject. How can you tell if you have become a know-it-all? Simple! You have stopped learning and growing in your area of specialization. You've stopped reading, listening to audios, and taking additional courses. The very act of failing to continue to seek out new information in your field means that you have unconsciously slipped into the intelligence trap of the low performer. You have unwittingly become a know-it-all by not continuing to learn and grow.

Albert Einstein once gave an advanced test to a graduate class of physics students at Princeton University. On the way back to his office, his graduate assistant asked him, "Dr. Einstein, wasn't that the same exam you gave to the physics class last year?" Dr. Einstein nodded and said, "Yes, it was the same test as last year." The graduate student summoned up his courage and asked, "But Dr. Einstein, how could you give the same test two years in a row?" "Because," Einstein replied, "in the last year, the answers have changed."

This story reminds us that the answers in your field are changing as you sit there. What was true a year ago may not be true today, and what is true today may not be true a year from now. The only way that you can be sure of being on top of your field is by continually taking in new information and comparing it with the information you have today.

> The greatest business breakthroughs take place as the result of the unexpected success or the unexpected failure.

In his book *Innovation and Entrepreneurship*, management guru Peter Drucker says that the greatest business breakthroughs take place as the result of the unexpected success or the unexpected failure. He goes on to explain that when something happens that is unusual or unexpected in your field, the person of average intelligence dismisses it as a random event or as an accident. The person of superior intelligence, irrespective of their IQ, looks upon each unexpected result as a sign of an underlying trend or warning of something to come.

For example, in 1975, IBM commissioned consultants to study the personal computer field. They came back with a conclusion that the market for personal computers was only a few hundred in the entire world at best. Because of this information, IBM decided to concentrate its efforts on mainframes where it was already the world leader and ignore the PC market, leaving it to a little upstart company in Cupertino, California, called Apple.

When Apple computers hit the market and began to sell by the hundreds and then the thousands, IBM did an about-face and decided to get seriously into the small computer business, and they did. They came up with a personal computer that within four years captured more than 50 percent of the world market for smaller computers, but IBM failed to notice that a major trend had taken place. Ignoring their success in personal computers, they continued to concentrate on the development and sale of mainframe computers. While their attention was focused on mainframes, more and more competitors rushed into the personal computer field, and eventually IBM was displaced. IBM failed to see that their special success in capturing 50 percent of the market reflected a sweeping trend in computers that would change the entire world. IBM scrambled to catch up, but it never did. Eventually it gave up, selling its personal computer division to Lenovo in 2005.

By the same token, there are changes taking place all around you today. Any one of them may indicate a trend that could lead to fortune and success for you. You must be open, awake, and alert to these changes. You must know in your heart that nothing remains the same very long and that your great opportunities will come from applying your knowledge and your brainpower to new products and new services.

All you need to start a fortune is an idea that is 10 percent new. All you need is something that is a little better, a little different, a little newer, a little faster, or of greater value than something else out there, and you can elbow your way to the front of the line. Many of the great fortunes being made today are being made by people who were penniless a few years ago until they came up with a breakthrough idea that they were able to unleash into the marketplace.

Two major factors stand in the way of unlocking your brainpower: *psychosclerosis* and *homeostasis*. Psychosclerosis is another name for a hardening of the attitudes. There is a particular type of mentality that is rigid, inflexible, and unchanging. It becomes settled into its attitudes and resists any attempt to change its mind. You probably know people who have this mechanical way of thinking.

The most successful people have the adaptive worldview.

On the other hand, the most successful people have the opposite: the adaptive worldview. They keep their minds open to new information. They refuse to close the book or engrave their ideas in stone. They're more concerned with what's right than who's right. They're willing to abandon an old idea if somebody else shows them a new idea has more merit. They're more in love with an idea that is right than they are with being right themselves.

Traits of Genius

Many studies of genius have made over the years. You can actually function at genius levels using these discoveries. One of the most remarkable conclusions is that geniuses are not necessarily people of extraordinarily high IQ. Geniuses seem to have certain characteristics in common, each of which you can develop and make into a regular part of your thinking. All geniuses seem to have open minds. They are curious, questioning, fluid, flexible, and willing to consider any possibilities. The adaptive mindset is like an open door that allows ideas to blow through from any direction and in any quantity. This is the mindset of the genius, and you can learn it.

The second quality of genius is that they all seem to approach problems and decisions systematically. They don't throw themselves at a problem like a dog chasing a car. Instead, they approach every difficult situation by asking structured questions. First of all, they ask why such a situation exists. How did it happen? Where and when did it first occur? Who is involved in it? What are the different ways that we could approach this situation? This active questioning opens your mind and expands your brainpower.

People with mechanical mindsets tend to jump to conclusions. They see a problem and immediately decide upon a solution. They're like people leaping from rock to rock, crossing a running brook. They don't stop and think that just because there is another rock there, that it is necessarily the right solution.

There's a direct relationship between the quantity of ideas and approaches you come up with in dealing with any situation and your likelihood of coming up with a high-quality idea that will really make a difference. You must continually resist the tendency to jump to conclusions or rush to judgment. You must hold back like a genius and keep asking questions. Keep your mind open. If something doesn't seem workable, ask how could it be made to work. What would you have to add to it or take away from it? What part of it would you have to do differently? Could you increase or decrease its size? The more you approach a problem or goal from different angles, the more likely you are to find a way up, over, around, or through it.

> You are an idea-generating organism.
> Creativity is your birthright.

You are an idea-generating organism. Creativity is your birthright. You are a highly intelligent individual with a continuous flow of good ideas that you can use to accomplish goals that you set for yourself. Even if you haven't used your creativity for a long time (and most people haven't), you can stir it up like sugar that has sunk to the bottom of a cup of coffee by revving up your creative mind with methods that I will talk about in the next chapter.

There's a law of probabilities with regard to creative thinking and tapping into your brainpower: the more ideas that you are exposed to, the more likely you are to be exposed to the right idea exactly when you need it. Successful people continually expose themselves to a flow of new ideas from a variety of sources. Unsuccessful people continue to recirculate the same tired old ideas with little imagination or creativity. For example, when you attend a seminar or lecture given by an expert who is sharing some of the most current ideas in his or her field, you'll get a continual bombardment of useful new insights. Many people's lives have been completely changed because they attended a single lecture given by a single intelligent person who gave them a single insight that was the key to their future.

Imagine what would happen if you attended courses, seminars, and lectures on a regular basis. You would be continually bombarding your mind with new ideas that would keep your mind dancing and keep your creative juices flowing.

Creative people read continually.

Creative people read continually, not only in their own fields, but in other fields as well. They read primarily nonfiction works. They subscribe to a variety of magazines and newspapers. They're continually scanning through the tables of contents and through critical articles. Always read with a red pen or a highlighter in your hand. Even better, learn how to speed-read so that you can go through material at 1,000 words a minute or better. Speed-reading is a skill like riding a bicycle that anyone can learn with a few hours of application. Thereafter, you'll be able to go through more information for the rest of your life than you imagined possible.

Effective people also make a habit of associating with other positive, creative people. They're constantly sharing ideas, cutting clippings out of magazines and newspapers, and passing them on to their friends to help them be more effective in their work and personal lives.

The Perils of Homeostasis

In addition to psychosclerosis, the second major factor that holds people back is *homeostasis*: striving to remain constant with what you've done and said in the past. Ralph Waldo Emerson once wrote that a foolish consistency is the hobgoblin of little minds. He adds individuals naturally try to remain consistent with what they might have done and said in the past, and it blocks off almost all possibilities for growth in the future. You should always be willing to abandon your old ideas just as fast as somebody else can prove that newer, better ideas are available.

One mental approach that you can use to enhance your mental potential is to be willing to admit that you are wrong. According to the research, fully 70 percent of all the decisions that you make in life will turn out to be wrong anyway—and this is an average. Some people's level of accuracy will be even worse, but you can assume for the time being that seven out of ten decisions that you make affecting your life and work will turn out to be wrong in the long run.

If 70 percent of the decisions that managers and executives make turn out to be wrong, how can the world continue to function? The answer is simple. Superior people, those who are in charge, are willing to cut their losses. They're willing to admit quickly that they've made a mistake and get out of the situation rather than persisting until it gets worse.

Unfortunately, most people fall in love with their past decisions. Once having made them, they're very reluctant to give them up even if all the evidence is against them. Don't be like this. Develop the habit of being the first to recognize that a decision that you may have made or conclusion that you may have reached has been invalidated or disproven by new information; drop the old decision and embrace the new way of doing things.

The most important single quality for success is flexibility.

The most important single quality for success in the twenty-first century is flexibility, particularly in your thinking. It is your willingness to chop and change and try new things. It especially means that you have the ability to continually abandon old, outmoded ideas in favor of new, more effective ones.

I've met many individuals over the years who spent almost all of their time arguing, rationalizing, and justifying doing things the old way even though it's perfectly clear to everyone that the old way no longer works.

Continual Learning Is Crucial

The turning point in my life came when as a young man in my early twenties, I learned that through personal development you can indeed pull yourself up by your own bootstraps. I discovered that by learning what you need to learn to achieve the goals that you set for yourself, there are virtually no limits on what you can do, have, or be. The future belongs to the competent. You could lose all of your money tomorrow, but as long as you maintain your brainpower, you can make it all back and more besides.

The future belongs to those who are better informed. The future belongs not to those who have more versus those who have less, but to those who know more versus those who know less. Furthermore, your information base is rapidly becoming obsolete, because information in your field is doubling every two to three years. Consequently, you must continually take in new information and ideas just to stay even.

Fortunately, there's a simple three-part program that you can use to keep ahead of the pack. I've used it and taught it to many thousands of people, and I have files full of letters from people whose entire lives have been changed as a result. The three keys to personal and professional development are continual reading, continual listening to audio learning programs, and continual training.

> ### Three Keys to Personal Development
> 1. Continual reading
> 2. Continual listening to audio programs
> 3. Continual training

To stay abreast of your field, you should read at least one hour per day, underlining and taking good notes; anything less than one hour per day will put you in a position of being passed by your competitors. My late friend, the inspirational speaker Jim Rohn, said that you should work at least as hard on yourself as you do on your job. At the very least, you should get up every morning and read for sixty minutes in your chosen field. Take careful notes, review the notes on a regular basis, reflect on what you have learned, and think about how you could apply it in your daily life. Use your powers of visualization to imagine yourself using the new information in some way. This will dramatically increase the speed at which you learn and retain the new ideas and the likelihood that you will use them at the first opportunity.

If you were to read just one hour per day, that would translate into about one book per week. One book per week will translate into about fifty books per year. Fifty books per year will translate into 500 books over the next ten years.

According to a 2022 Gallup poll, the average American reads 12.6 books per year, including ones they have not finished, and have finished only 5.38 books per year. Thirty-three percent of high-school graduates never read another book again. Meanwhile, in the information age, if you you're not reading continually, you are in serious danger of being made obsolete by the passage of time. If you read one hour per day, one book per week, you'll be getting the equivalent of a PhD in your field every year. You'll become one of the smartest, best informed, and most productive people in your business.

I encouraged a good friend to read daily for two or three years. He'd gotten out of the habit of reading after he left school. He argued that reading wasn't that important. Meanwhile, he struggled to make a living. He was continually frustrated. He was continually bested in his sales by his competitors. Finally, he gave in, and he began to read just a little. He was amazed at how helpful the reading was and how much better informed he was when he spoke to his clients. He soon began reading as I had recommended: an hour per day, a book per week. After a year, his income had doubled. After two years, his income doubled again. Today, he's one of the highest-paid people in his field. Every time I see him, he's proud to tell me that he seldom meets a client who is as knowledgeable as he is about their field, and the more he reads, the more competent and confident he feels.

> To earn more, you must learn more.

To earn more, you must learn more. You cannot move ahead except to the degree to which you learn and practice something new.

The second key to continual learning is audio learning programs. If you travel in your work, you probably spend 500 to 1,000 hours per year in your car. If you turn this driving time into learning time, you'll get the equivalent of three to six months of forty-hour weeks of learning just driving around. I have met countless people who have doubled, tripled, and quadrupled their income by actively listening to audio learning programs.

The third key to continual learning and unlocking your mental potential is to take all the training you can get.

If a training program makes it into the public arena, the person giving the training program has probably gotten many years of experience and may have spent hundreds of hours assembling the programs that you can take in a half or a full day. You can sometimes save yourself weeks, months, and even years of hard work by attending a seminar given by an expert who explains state-of-the-art ways to get your job done faster and better.

When you combine these three—regular reading, regular listening to audio learning programs, and continual training—you have a dynamite combination that can propel you forward at a greater speed than you ever could go without them.

It's been said that knowledge is power. In fact, it is only knowledge that can be applied to practical purposes for someone else that is actually power. To unlock your mental potential, you must continually fill your mind with new ideas. You must stay current with your field. You must regularly associate with other leading people in your area of specialization. You must be continually looking for ways to do what you do better, faster, cheaper, and easier for your clients and customers. You must stay on the cutting edge of your field so that you are and you continue to be one of the most valuable people in your business.

Fortunately, in the information age, knowledge is everything, and the amount of knowledge that you can gather is limited only by your own personal application. There are really no limits on what you can accomplish except for the limits you set on yourself. The more you learn, the more you earn. The more knowledgeable you become about your field, the more courage and confidence you have to implement your skills, and the more courage and confidence you have, the higher will be your self-esteem and your sense of personal power.

Key Points in This Chapter

1. The primary source of value today is knowledge, information, and ideas.
2. Small differences in the way you think can lead to tremendous differences in performance.
3. Failing to seek out new information is slipping into the intelligence trap of the low performer.
4. A brilliant individual sees an unexpected result as a sign of an underlying trend or a warning of something to come.
5. Two factors that stand in the way of brainpower are psychosclerosis and homeostasis.
6. The more ideas you generate and are exposed to, the more likely you are to hit on the right solution.
7. Three steps to remaining current: continual reading, continual listening to audio programs, and continual training.
8. The amount of knowledge that you can gather is limited only by your own personal application.

four

You Are a Genius

Every change in your life will come about as the result of your current thinking—your mind colliding with a new idea. Ideas are the keys to the future. They contain the answers to all of your problems and the ways to achieve all of your goals. You need to become an idea generator so that you are continually coming up with new and better ideas to deal with the continuous changes and opportunities taking place around you.

Fortunately, as I've already pointed out, you are naturally creative. It is an innate quality. You are born with it, but it is subject to the law of use. If you don't use it, you lose it (at least temporarily), but you can reignite your creativity by doing certain things in certain ways, such as the methods that I'm talking about here.

Every person who accomplishes anything worthwhile begins with a big dream or a vision of what is possible for them. They ignore their current surroundings, situations, and problems; instead, they imagine themselves sometime in the future, living the kind of life they would like to live.

You need to do the same on a regular basis. In chapter 1, I talked about your ideal future vision. This is where you project forward five years and imagine that all of your dreams have come true. What would it look like? Where would you be? Who would be there with you? What would you be doing? How much would you be earning? Be as specific as you can. You then think back to the present day and you think of all the things you could do to capitalize on your opportunities and overcome or compensate for your limitations and obstacles. This is the primary use of creative thinking: to solve problems and bring breakthroughs to accelerate your progress toward the things that are most important to you.

Three Factors of Creativity

1. Intensely desired goals
2. Pressing problems
3. Focused questions

Intensely Desired Goals

Three key factors trigger creativity. You can use all of them continually in everything you do. They are: (1) intensely desired goals, (2) pressing problems, and (3) focused questions. When you bring all three of them to bear, your mind begins to function at an amazing speed, producing ideas and insights of tremendous value.

You actually have three minds working for you. Most people use their conscious minds most of the time and only use their subconscious minds for the autonomic functions of eating, sleeping, working, basic memory, and so on. Your third mind is your superconscious mind, a mind that contains all the ideas and answers you'll ever need to achieve any goal.

> Your superconscious mind contains all the ideas and answers you'll ever need to achieve any goal.

By using the three methods of mental activation—goals, problems, and questions—you trigger all three of your minds simultaneously, and you begin to function at much higher levels than the average person.

The first thing that you require is clear, specific goals. Your goals need to be written and rewritten over and over again. In fact, one of the most powerful exercises you can use to activate your creative powers is to rewrite your goals in the present tense each morning. Get a spiral notebook. Each morning after your daily reading, take a few minutes and rewrite your major goals in the present tense, as if they already existed.

Take a few seconds after rewriting your goals and visualize them as a part of your reality. Actually see them in your mind as if they already existed. Then smile, relax, and let go. This method of rewriting your goals, visualizing them, and then letting them go with complete confidence that they will materialize exactly when you're ready for them is extremely powerful.

It not only passes your goal on to your subconscious mind, but it also activates your superconscious mind and begins attracting into your life the people and circumstances that can help you to achieve it.

Emotion is the key. The more intensely you desire a goal, the more rapidly it materializes. Intense emotion is like stepping on the accelerator of your mental computer: it causes your mind to race. The more positive, excited, and enthusiastic you are about achieving anything, the more rapidly your mind goes to work to bring it into your life.

Another use of emotion is to calmly, confidently, and happily imagine yourself enjoying the feeling that you would have if your goal were already a part of your life. For example, if you want to earn more money and achieve a higher position in life, imagine that you're already there. Imagine how you would feel. Close your eyes and get the feeling of happiness, joy, and inner satisfaction that you would experience if you were already successful. When you can combine a clear mental picture of your goal with the same emotion that you would have if it were achieved, you activate the higher powers of your mind that trigger your creativity. These powers will then bring you insights and ideas that will help you to achieve your goal far faster.

Pressing Problems

The second factor that triggers your creativity and activates your positive mind is pressing problems. Most people do not understand the true nature of problems. They are normal, necessary, and unavoidable. Problems come unbidden in spite of your best efforts to avoid them. The only part of problems over which you have any control is your response to them. Successful, happy people respond positively and constructively to problems. In this way, they demonstrate that they have developed high levels of responsibility in the literal sense: they respond effectively when things happen to them that are unexpected or undesired.

The more pressing your problems and the more emotion you invest in solving them, the more creative you'll become.

The key to activating your creativity in problem solving is to define them clearly in writing. Whatever difficulties, obstacles, challenges, or factors that are hindering you, define them clearly in writing. Sometimes when you write down a problem, you'll find that it is actually a cluster problem; it's made of several smaller problems. You then define the main problem and define its individual parts separately. Sometimes solving one part of the problem leads to the solution of the entire situation.

If you're not earning the kind of money that you would like, that is an unsolved problem. A goal unachieved is an unsolved problem. An unexpected reversal or setback is a problem. In every case, your job is to not let the problem get on top of you, but to get on top of the problem.

If I asked you what you did for a living, you would tell me what your current position or job description is, but whatever it is, what you do for a living is really to solve problems. You are a professional problem solver. If there were no problems in your work, you would have no job. When people become unable to solve the problems created by their work, they're quickly replaced by people who can. When you become an excellent problem solver, you are quickly promoted to solving even bigger and more important problems.

What you do for a living is solve problems.

In any event, you are a problem solver.

The only question is whether or not you are good at solving problems. Your job is to become excellent at solving any issue that the world can throw at you.

Focused Questions

The third key to activating your creativity is focused questions. Well-worded, focused, provocative, challenging questions activate your mind, like sticking an electric prod in your side. The best consultants often don't give answers; instead, they force their clients to ask and answer tough questions. When you want to trigger your own creativity, you have to ask yourself some tough questions as well.

Remember zero-based thinking? Keep asking yourself, "If I were not now doing this, knowing what I now know, would I begin?" You will be amazed at how creative you become when you look at every aspect of your life as though you could choose to start it again if you wanted to based on your current knowledge or experience.

Sometimes the answer to your biggest dilemma is simply to walk away altogether. Sometimes the answer is to simply abandon a course of action that isn't working out.

Some other questions that you can use to trigger your creativity: What am I trying to do? Whenever you experience any frustration or resistance, ask yourself, how am I trying to do it? What are your assumptions? What are your obvious assumptions, and what are your unconscious assumptions? What are you assuming to be true that, if it were not true, would change your thinking altogether?

> ### Three Questions for a New Product or Service
> 1. Is there a market?
> 2. Is the market big enough?
> 3. Is the market concentrated enough?

Marketing as a Problem

When I consult with a company that's trying to market a new product or service and is having difficulties in the marketplace, I ask them what the problems are. They give me a whole list of difficulties with advertising, promotion, sales, distribution, delivery, and service, but I know that the bottom line is that their sales are not high enough, so I ask them these three questions.

These are questions that you can ask when considering any new potential product or service for any market. The first question is, is there a market? Is there a market of people who can and will buy this product or service in competition with other products and services currently being offered? Many people start businesses without realizing how hard it is to attract a customer away from another supplier if the customer's already happy with his or her current situation. The customer is in his or her own comfort zone in that area.

If the answer is yes, there's definitely a market, my next question is, is the market large enough? Many products and services are good, valuable, and worthwhile, but there's not a large enough market for potential high profitability.

Many people—especially in entrepreneurial ventures—go broke because the market is simply not large enough to justify the trouble of producing the product or service in the first place. Every investment must be compared with every other possible investment at the same time. There may be a lot of other, more profitable places to put your time and money.

> Invest yourself so that you get the highest return on energy.

With regard to personal strategic planning, your job is to invest yourself so that you get the highest return on energy. There are a thousand different ways that you can spend your time and your life—which are your most valuable resources—and you must always invest it where you can get the highest return.

The third question I ask my clients is, is the market concentrated enough so that you can advertise and sell to it in a cost-effective way? This final question often sinks a new product idea. Yes, there is a market, and yes, the market is large enough, but the market is spread over such a wide geographical area that it is virtually impossible to sell to it effectively.

The Theory of Constraints

Another factor that is extremely helpful in triggering creative ideas is contained in the *theory of constraints*. In every activity, whatever you want to do, there are constraints or bottlenecks that determine how fast you get from where you are to where you want to go. The act of sitting down and identifying the critical constraints in your environment often triggers ideas and insights that help you to alleviate them.

For example, take the goal of doubling your income over the next three to five years. Why isn't your income double already? Why aren't you already earning twice as much as you're earning today? What's holding you back? Of all the things that are holding you back, what's the major factor that is constraining your forward motion?

The 80/20 rule seems to apply to constraints. In this context, this rule says that 80 percent of the constraints that are holding you back from achieving your goals are within you. Only 20 percent are in the outside world. Most people think that their major problems lie in the situations and circumstances around them, but this is usually untrue. Most of the reasons you are not moving ahead have to do with your own lack of skills, abilities, or personality traits.

Say you are in sales. You want to double your income in the next three to five years, if not sooner. The critical constraint is the amount of your product or service that you sell.

Once you've identified this main constraint, you ask, what is the constraint behind that? This next constraint may be in the number of prospects that you have to talk to. Again, look behind that constraint and ask, what constraint is causing this limitation? It may be your ability to prospect—something that is inside of you rather than in the marketplace. One good way to test whether the constraint is internal or external is to look around you and see if anyone else is accomplishing the same goals that you want to accomplish. Is anyone else already earning twice as much as you are earning by selling the same product or service in the same market? If someone is already doing it, then the constraint is internal, not external. It is something inside you. It is the lack of a particular ability or attribute that you need to overcome.

They say that when a man's fight begins with himself, he is really worth something. The superior person always asks the question, what is it in me that is holding me back? Superior people always look to themselves first. It may very well be that there is something in your outside world that is acting as the break on your potentialities, but the place to start looking is inside; the odds are, you'll find it there.

With these triggers, you are on your way to turning up your creative capacity, like turning up the light in a dark room with a dimmer switch. When you set clear goals that you have a burning desire to achieve, combined with pressing problems that you have clearly defined, and focused questions that provoke your thinking, you can then identify the key constraints and go to work to alleviate them. Sometimes the removal of one key constraint with an idea that you generate can put you onto the high road toward achieving your most important goals.

Ten Forms of Intelligence

1. Verbal
2. Mathematical
3. Physical
4. Musical
5. Visual and spatial
6. Interpersonal
7. Intrapersonal
8. Entrepreneurial
9. Intuitive
10. Abstract and conceptual

Your Multiple Intelligences

Throughout your schooling, you were tested only on the basis of your verbal and mathematical intelligence, but recent research indicates that you have a variety of intelligences, in any one of which you could be a genius and which in combination could allow you to accomplish extraordinary things. Your main job is to identify your predominant form of intelligence or intelligences and then apply yourself using it to achieve what you want.

> Your main job is to identify your predominant form of intelligence.

Your first form of intelligence is *verbal*. This is your ability to speak, your command of language. This ability to understand and to use language well is closely associated with success in any field that involves communication with others.

Your second intelligence is *mathematical*. This is your ability to use numbers skillfully to add, subtract, divide, and multiply. It's your ability to read financial statements and develop financial ratios. It's your ability to develop pro forma statements that enable you to analyze the pros or cons of a particular investment or expenditure.

Your third form of intelligence is *physical*. This is the intelligence enjoyed by top athletes, who have extraordinary abilities of timing and coordination in the movement and use of their bodies. A person could fail in school on verbal and mathematical tests and still be an extraordinary success athletically, even though it would never show up on a report card.

Your fourth form of intelligence is *musical*. A Mozart or a Beethoven could have been poor at sports and poor in school and yet contributed classical music that rings down the ages. Many musicians today who are at the top of their fields did poorly in conventional school subjects, but they have an exceptional ability to create and express music.

Your fifth form of intelligence is *visual and spatial* intelligence: the ability to see shapes and forms and patterns. An architect, an engineer, a painter, or a person who has developed the capacity to visualize clearly would have this intelligence. An architect, for example, might be able to develop, first in their mind and then on paper, beautiful buildings that people with higher levels of mathematical intelligence would be able to convert into blueprints and exact dimensions for construction.

Your sixth form of intelligence is *interpersonal*. This is the highest-paid form of intelligence in America. The highest-paid salespeople, businesspeople, professionals, consultants, and politicians have very high levels of interpersonal intelligence. This may be your particular area of genius as well. It's the ability to communicate, negotiate, influence, and persuade other people. It consists of a high degree of sensitivity to the moods, thoughts, and feelings of others and the ability to interact with them effectively to get things done both with and through them. Good managers, team leaders, and salespeople usually have interpersonal intelligence developed to a very high degree. As a result, people want to work with them and cooperate with them in the purchase or sale of products and in the accomplishment of group goals.

Your seventh form of intelligence is *intrapersonal*: an advanced ability to be extremely aware of yourself, know exactly what you want and what you don't want, and set goals and make plans for their accomplishment. People with high levels of intrapersonal intelligence spend a good deal of time reflecting on how they're thinking and feeling. They know themselves better and so are more effective in dealing with others.

Your eighth form of intelligence is *entrepreneurial* intelligence. This is the ability to see market opportunities and combine various resources together to produce products and services that can be sold at a profit. Entrepreneurial intelligence is one of the highest-paid forms in our society today and is the foundation of all successful fast-growing businesses.

Your ninth form of intelligence is *intuitive*: the ability to sense the rightness or wrongness of a situation, to judge people quickly and accurately, and to come up with ideas and insights using your intuitive abilities.

Your tenth form of intelligence is *abstract* or *conceptual* intelligence. This is the kind of intelligence possessed by an Einstein, who could see himself riding on a beam of light. As a result, he was able to formulate the theory of relativity, which completely revolutionized twentieth-century physics. There may be still more forms of intelligence than these. At any rate, you can imagine that these ten intelligences are like the digits from zero through nine. If you take any large city, you will find that there are hundreds of thousands of people with different telephone numbers, even though all of their telephone numbers are made up of seven of those ten digits.

It's the same with you.

Your unique combination of intelligences, especially your seven best forms, make up a kind of personal intellectual telephone number that makes you different from every other person and capable of performing at extraordinary levels. You need to identify your intelligences, be aware of them, and respect them. You need to develop a high level of faith and confidence in your ability to use your mental powers to overcome any obstacle and achieve any goal.

> Identify your intelligences, be aware of them, and respect them.

You also have three ways of learning: *auditory*, *visual*, and *kinesthetic*. You can learn by listening, by seeing, or by feeling and movement. Each person learns using all three, but each person also has a preferred learning style. When you combine your dominant intelligences with your preferred method of learning, you create a combination of intelligence and ability that can enable you to achieve remarkable things.

Mindstorming: The Twenty-Idea Method

There are two powerful methods that you can use to unlock your brainpower and to generate ideas for goal achievement: *mindstorming* and *brainstorming*. The first will make you rich, and the second will enable you to tap into the brainpower of other people.

Mindstorming, or the *twenty-idea method*, is so powerful that using it will change your life. I learned it from inspirational speaker Earl Nightingale many years ago, and I've taught it to many tens of thousands of people. I've never found a person who has not seen profound improvements in any area to which this method was applied. Once you start using it, it will work for you very quickly and easily. This is how it goes.

Take a blank sheet of paper and write your current problem or goal at the top of the page in the form of a question. Again, let us say your goal is to double your income. Try to make the question as specific as possible. The more specific the question, the better your mind can focus on it and the better answers you will generate. Instead of saying, how can I make more money? you would say, what can I do to double my income over the next twenty-four months? Write this down at the top of the page.

Then generate twenty different answers to that question. Force yourself to write out twenty different things that you can think of doing, either immediately or later, that would enable you to double your income. For example, you would probably start off with simple answers, as most people do. You could write "work harder," "work longer," "upgrade my education," "improve my skills" in a specific area, and so on.

After the first three to five simple answers, it will start to get tougher.

The second five answers will be harder, and the last ten answers will be like squeezing water out of a stone, but you must force yourself to stay at the piece of paper until you have answered the question with at least twenty different answers. You can play with these answers if you like. For example, you may decide to write the exact opposite of one of your earlier answers.

You can also come up with ridiculous answers. For example, someone might say, "Work harder at my current job." The next answer might be, "Work less hard at a different job," or "Create your own job," or "Get a second-income job." If your income depends upon selling and your success in selling depends upon prospecting, your answer could be to double the number of qualified prospects that you see each week, or it could be to see higher-potential prospects, who have the ability to buy twice as much of your product, or it could be to sell a different product with a higher commission per sale.

In any case, the potential answers are limited only by your imagination. Your capacity to generate ideas to help you is, to all intents and purposes, infinite.

Once you've answered the question with at least twenty answers (and you can write more, if they come to you), go back over the answers and select at least one solution to be implemented immediately. This is extremely important. Your willingness to take action keeps the flow of ideas running through your mind once you've generated them in the first place.

A friend of mine recently told me of a variation on this exercise. He said that once he had generated his twenty ideas and selected the one he was going to implement immediately, he performed the twenty-idea method on that new idea, generating twenty different ways to put that idea to work.

You can do the first or both of these mindstorming exercises if you like, but once you've implemented the first idea, you'll begin coming up with other ideas as well. If you do this exercise in the morning before you start out, you'll find yourself thinking creatively all day long. Your mind will be fast, sharp, and alert. You'll see solutions to problems and obstacles as fast as they come up.

If you do this exercise every day for just five days, you'll generate a hundred new ideas to help you achieve your goals. By practicing mindstorming on a regular basis, you will soon have so many good ideas that there will not be enough hours in the day to carry them out.

More people have become rich using this process than any other method of creative thinking ever known to man. The only thing it requires is your willingness to use mindstorming regularly and apply the ideas you generate until this becomes a regular habit for you.

Brainstorming

The second form of creative thinking for unlocking your brainpower is a method you can use with two or more people. It's called *brainstorming*, and is a form of mindstorming done in a group, but it has slightly different rules.

Brainstorming was originally developed by Alex Osborn and first described in his 1946 book, *Applied Imagination*. It has since proliferated and is used all over the world in every type of organization to generate a variety of options to any problem. I've personally taught brainstorming to thousands of the executives and staff of some of the world's largest corporations. It's a very simple process.

The ideal number of people in a brainstorming session is from four to seven. Below four, you don't have enough minds to generate a large enough variety of different approaches, and above seven, it becomes too unwieldy and people don't get a chance to contribute.

> The critical part of brainstorming is that no evaluation of the ideas takes place during the brainstorming session itself.

The critical part of brainstorming is that no evaluation of the ideas takes place during the brainstorming session itself. The session is entirely focused on generating the greatest quantity of ideas possible within a short period of time. The ideal length for brainstorming sessions varies from fifteen to forty-five minutes.

One job of managers and team leaders is to sit their staff down on a regular basis to brainstorm certain problems. Just call everyone in and announce that you're going to brainstorm a particular goal or situation for 15 minutes; then everyone will go back to work. You'll be amazed at the results.

There are two key players in a brainstorming session. The first is the leader. The leader's job is to encourage everyone to contribute as much as possible. One of the best ways to lead a brainstorming session is to go around the table and encourage each person to throw in an idea, almost like playing cards, where you encourage each person to bet or pass. Once you've gone around the table a couple of times, people will start generating ideas at a rapid rate.

The second key function in a brainstorming session is that of the recorder. This is a person who writes down the ideas as they're generated. In some brainstorming sessions, everyone starts with a stack of index cards in front of them, and as they generate an idea, they write it down and throw it into the center. At the end of the session, all the ideas are gathered up for evaluation later. Start and stop the brainstorming session exactly on time, no matter how well it's going. Then gather up all the ideas and take them away to be reviewed at a later time.

In some brainstorming exercises, we use index cards, and we break the group up into smaller groups. Each of the smaller groups will generate ideas and answers to a single question. Afterwards, the index cards are collected, shuffled, and handed out to the groups completely mixed up.

In the second phase of the exercise, each group is asked to take the cards they have and evaluate them, judging them in terms of their value prior to reporting back to the group. In a session with twenty or thirty people, 200 or 300 ideas can be generated, which can be organized, evaluated, and reported. The results are astonishing. I've worked with companies that have come up with so many solutions to problems that they didn't have enough hours in the day or enough people to apply them all.

By the way, if you're in a good relationship with another person, you form an excellent brainstorming team. A husband and wife or even two friends together can be excellent at brainstorming as long as they don't attempt to evaluate the ideas at the same time that they're generating them. What kills a brainstorming session is the tendency of people to criticize the ideas as they're generated. As soon as one person's ideas are criticized, the brainstorming session shuts off. No one wants to stick their neck out. No one wants to be humiliated or ridiculed in front of others. That is why it's so important to concentrate on the number of ideas and leave the evaluation of the ideas to another time or to other people.

The most important part of unlocking your mental potential and harnessing the genius that lies within you is, first of all, to accept that you are extremely intelligent. Next, use the methods mentioned above to generate ideas for achieving your goals. There's something exciting and uplifting about coming up with ideas that help you. The more ideas you generate, the more energy and enthusiasm you have. The more energy and enthusiasm you have, the more confident you will be. By unlocking your mental abilities, you will set ever greater goals and accomplish ever more wonderful things, because you really are a genius.

Key Points in This Chapter

1. You are naturally and innately creative.
2. Three factors of creativity: intensely desired goals, pressing problems, and focused questions.
3. There are three aspects of mind: conscious, subconscious, and superconscious.
4. Three questions for a new product or service: (1) Is there a market? (2) Is the market big enough? (3) Is the market concentrated enough?
5. The theory of constraints: there are constraints or bottlenecks that determine how fast you get from where you are to where you want to go.
6. Each of us is a unique combination of the ten types of intelligence.
7. Mindstorming and brainstorming will develop new ideas for any problem or question.
8. During brainstorming, no evaluation of the ideas is to take place during the session itself.

five

The Keys to Wealth Building

If you want to learn how to cook, you study cooking. If you want to be a lawyer, you study law. If you want to be an engineer or an architect, you study engineering or architecture, and if you want to be financially successful, you study others who have become financially successful. You find out what they did, and you do the same things over and over until you get the same results.

Perhaps the most important principle of success was first articulated by Greek philosophers in antiquity: the law of cause and effect. It says that for every effect, there are specific causes. Everything happens for a reason. Success is not an accident. What happens to you is not determined by luck or by coincidence.

When I began my upward journey from poverty and frustration to financial independence and self-confidence, I decided to study the most successful people in our society and find out what they had done to get there. I learned some amazing things that have helped me over the years, and I'm going to share them with you.

The first thing I learned is that there are millions of millionaires in the United States (approximately 24.5 million as of 2024), most of whom are self-made. These are men and women who have started with nothing, often broke or deeply in debt, and have gradually built themselves up to the point where they're financially independent. These men and women have come from every walk of life, with every level of education and skill, with every difficulty, obstacle, handicap, and challenge that you could dream of.

Some are young, and some are old. Some are new immigrants who started off with no language skills, and some have been in America for generations. Some have excellent educations from the finest universities, and some are high-school dropouts. Some have superb physical health; others have been in wheelchairs, been hard of hearing, blind, or had other physical limitations. No matter what problems are holding you back, someone else—probably thousands of other people—have had problems far worse than you could ever dream of, yet they've gone on to be successful nonetheless, and so can you.

The late Thomas J. Stanley spent decades studying self-made millionaires. He interviewed thousands of them and compiled his findings into a variety of books, research, studies, and reports, including *The Millionaire Next Door* and *The Millionaire Mind*. He concluded that every kind of person, from every walk of life, has been able to start from nothing and pass the magic million-dollar marker by doing certain things in a certain way over and over again.

When I began studying self-made millionaires, I was living in a rented apartment with rented furniture. I had a car that wasn't paid for, and I was deeply in debt. I was between jobs and living off of credit cards.

After several years of applying what I had learned about other successful people, hour after hour, day after day and month after month, my financial fortunes began to turn. Within a few years, I had managed to solve my financial problems. When I look back, I've found that all I really did was to learn what other successful people had done before me and then do the same things.

There are a lot of myths about self-made millionaires in America. If you want to become a self-made millionaire, you need to dispel some of these myths in your own mind. As humorist Will Rogers said, "It isn't what we don't know that gives us trouble, it's what we know that ain't so."

Fixed ideas that are holding you back may be completely untrue, but they will cut off your chances of success nonetheless. Many people feel that you have to have a great education, start off with a lot of money, and be in an ideal situation to become financially successful. All of these are false. In fact, in a survey of the Forbes 400—the 400 richest men and women in the United States—high-school dropouts among the group were found to be worth on average $300 million more than university graduates.

The Reality Principle

The much-admired late president of General Electric Corporation, Jack Welch, said that the most important single quality of leadership is the reality principle. The reality principle says that you must deal with the world as it is, not as you wish it would be. You must be completely honest with yourself. You must refuse to engage in self-delusion and in hoping that things will work out whether or not you do anything about them. With regard to building wealth in your life, you must be brutally honest and frank with yourself. You cannot play any games with your own head. You cannot wish and hope and pray that somehow you're going to win the lottery or strike it rich as the result of luck or some external circumstance.

Everything that you ever become is completely up to you. The good news is that in America, there are more opportunities for wealth and affluence than have ever existed in all of human history, and as information technology and competition expands and explodes, more and more opportunities are being created every single day for the creative minority. Your job is to find them and exploit them.

> There are currently more opportunities for wealth and affluence than have existed in all of human history.

Most self-made millionaires start off with little or nothing. They save their money carefully over a long period of time until they have enough to start a small enterprise or business. Some of the biggest companies in America were started on a kitchen table or in a garage, including the Hewlett Packard Corporation and Apple Corporation.

In Dr. Thomas Stanley's studies of self-made millionaires, he found that the number one quality that they used to explain their success was hard work. Self-made millionaires work hard. They start earlier, they work harder, and they stay later. Self-made millionaires work an average of fifty-nine hours per week. The average working person in America today works about thirty-five hours per week, even though they are paid for about forty.

According to the studies, fully 50 percent of all working time is wasted. Even most managers privately report that half of the time they spend at work is spent doing things that have nothing whatever to do with the job. The most common opportunities for time wastage at work are idle socializing with coworkers, personal telephone calls, and personal business, combined with starting a little later, long coffee breaks and lunch hours, and leaving a little earlier.

Only about 5 percent of people working today are working from the time they begin until the time they finish. They, of course, are the ones on the fast track in their careers.

The research also found that the other 50 percent of the time that people are actually working on company tasks and responsibilities, they tend to work on low-value, low-priority tasks and therefore get very little done. Today, we're seeing layoffs of thousands of men and women from large corporations. An average of 1,287,000 men and women were laid off per year from 2020 to 2024. The tech sector has been especially hard-hit: "Big players like Meta, Amazon, Microsoft, Google, TikTok, and Salesforce let go of around 25,000 employees" in the first four weeks of 2024 alone, reports *Forbes*.

Why? The answer is complex (overhiring after the pandemic, cost cutting, mergers), but it is at least in part because the companies have finally learned that they have been paying high salaries to people who are producing low value. No company can survive very long under those conditions, and these companies are determined to survive, so the redundant staff have to go.

If you're serious about becoming financially independent or (even better) becoming a self-made millionaire, I can tell you two things. First, it is eminently possible. Hundreds of thousands of men and women achieve it on a regular basis, and whatever anyone else has done, you can probably do as well. The fact that someone else has done it is ample evidence that it's possible for you. The only question is, how badly do you want it? Second, the reality principle says that if you want to achieve a certain level of success, you have to find out what successful people have done and then do the same things over and over until you get the same results. As long as you don't try to fool yourself and look for shortcuts, you are virtually guaranteed to eventually reach and even exceed your goals.

> If you want to achieve success, find out what successful people have done and then do those things.

The Forty-Plus Formula

You can start off with what I call the *forty-plus formula*.

This says that you work forty hours per week for survival. If you only work forty hours per week—if you only work the number of hours that are required of you—all you will ever do is survive. You will tread water. You'll make enough to pay your bills and perhaps a little more, but you'll never get ahead and you'll never be successful. If you happen to lose your job, you'll be in serious difficulties.

According to the surveys, a huge number of Americans have no discretionary income: with every paycheck, they spend every penny they earn and a little bit more besides. Many American families have little or no savings. The average American household has a median account balance of some $8,000, according to CNN.

Your job is to beat the odds. Your job is to find out what unsuccessful people do and *don't* do it. At the same time, your job is to find out what successful people do and do those things over and over again until you become successful as well.

Find out what unsuccessful people do and *don't* do it.

According to my forty-plus formula, every hour that you put in over forty hours on your job or on yourself is an investment in your future success. You can tell exactly where you're going to be five years from now by simply looking at how many hours per week you put in on your job and on improving your ability to get results for your employer and your customers. If you work fifty hours per week, you're putting yourself on the side of the angels. The average self-made millionaire in America, as I said, works fifty-nine hours per week in America, and in many cases, for many years he or she works seventy and even eighty hours per week.

I've studied successful men and women for decades. I have never found a single one who works only forty hours, five days per week. Successful people work six days per week. They work ten hours per day, six days per week, and they do it for many months and many years. The average self-made millionaire has taken twenty-two years to get from the point of being broke to the point of being worth more than $1 million. It is not easy, and it's not quick, but it is eminently possible if you want it badly enough.

Work All the Time You Work

The second part of success is perhaps the most important: work all the time you work. This is a remarkable idea for many people. They look upon work as an extension of school. You go to school to socialize and spend time with your friends between classes. When they take their first job, many people think it is a place to spend time with your friends. This is why fully half of the working day is spent socializing and in idle conversation on the telephone with friends and family. Many people see work as a giant sandbox where they go to play, do a few things, get a paycheck, and go home—but this is not for you. You must work all the time you work. When you go to work, you put your head down, and for the entire time that you are there, you work wholeheartedly.

> Work all the time you work.

Many people believe the myth that you have to spend a lot of time getting along with your coworkers. Of course it's important to be a positive and pleasant person to work with, but you can do this in a few minutes each day. You don't have to spend endless hours of socializing over recent sports activities, television shows, and family experiences. Your job is to work all the time you work.

When you go into work in the morning, you don't pick up your dry cleaning or drop off your laundry. You don't socialize with your friends or phone your family. You don't take long coffee breaks and lunch hours. You work all the time you work. You put your head down and you commit yourself to getting the most done that you possibly can in the time available to you. If someone else comes in to talk to you, you explain that you would be pleased to talk to them after work, but right now you have to get back to work.

Keep repeating to yourself, "Back to work, back to work, back to work." Get the reputation as being the hardest-working person in the organization. People who achieve great financial success either in their own businesses or working for other organizations are people who very early develop a reputation for hard work (and everyone knows who works the hardest in every organization, including your own). No quality will bring you to more the attention of people who can help you than developing a reputation for being one of the hardest workers around.

A young man told me how he started off with a large organization and eventually passed all the people who were ahead of him. He noticed that his boss came in a little earlier than the rest of the staff and stayed to finish up his work and left a little bit later, so he resolved to come in fifteen minutes before his boss came in and to leave fifteen minutes afterwards. He put his resolution into action immediately. (This is another hallmark of the high achiever: they don't procrastinate when they have a good idea.) He began coming in fifteen minutes before his boss and spending the whole day working all the time he worked. When his boss left, he would still be there working.

High achievers don't procrastinate when they have a good idea.

The boss said nothing for several weeks. Finally, he came over to the young man and asked him why he always seemed to be there. Every time the boss came or left, this young man was at his desk working away. Why? The young man said it was because he was determined to be successful in this company, and he knew he couldn't be successful unless he was willing to work harder than anyone else. The boss smiled and nodded and went on his way. Within a year, the young man had been given additional responsibilities, each one of which he took on and fulfilled completely. He was soon promoted to a higher position. He studied, upgraded his skills, and continued to work hard. Within a couple of years, he had surpassed all of his rivals. He had earned the respect and esteem of the other managers, and they soon promoted him so that he was one of them rather than one of the staff. It's a simple strategy, but one that works over and over again.

Add Value

If your goal is to achieve wealth in your lifetime, you have to know how it is done. It is contained in two words: "add value." All wealth comes from adding value in some way: from serving and satisfying customers better than they could be served by someone else, by adding value that no one else is currently adding. For your entire career, your job is to constantly seek out ways of adding value for your boss, your coworkers, customers, suppliers, and everyone else on whom you rely for your success. This should become your mantra: *add value, add value, add value.*

All wealth comes from adding value.

In your job, you should be looking for ways every day, every week, to add value: to become more valuable than you were before. A major revolution in thought has taken place in the world of work in the last few years: it is the idea that you must justify your position anew each day. It used to be that people could coast. They would work hard for a few years until they'd reach a certain position of responsibility, and then they would coast for many years. They would say, "I did a great job for a few years, so now I'm entitled to keep on at my same level." This is no longer good enough. Today, everybody wants to know, what have you done for me lately? Your boss wants to know what you have done to add value this day, this week.

Time and Speed

There are two major sources of value in the world of work today: time and knowledge. I've already discussed knowledge. Time is the currency of modern business. Everyone is fixated on reducing the amount of time that it takes to get the same results. Customers will pay dearly for anyone who can save them time in getting them the products and services that they want and need to improve their work and their lives. Most of the major improvements in modern management are aimed at reducing the amount of time that it takes to get critical results.

The most important factor of time today is speed. The most important quality that you can develop with regard to time is a sense of urgency: a determination to move fast when opportunity presents itself. Develop a bias for action. Fast tempo is essential to success.

Successful people work hard, and they work fast. Procrastination is not only the thief of time, it's the thief of life. Develop a habit of moving quickly when something needs to be done. Develop a reputation for speed and dependability. Study after study shows that people with the best reputations for speed and dependability quickly move onto the fast track in their careers. The wonderful thing is that the faster you move, the better you get. The faster you move, the more experience you get, the more you learn, the more competent you become, and the more energy and enthusiasm you have. People who move fast have a totally different temperament and personality than people who move slowly or who take a casual attitude toward their work.

Do it now!

One way to dramatically accelerate the speed at which you get the job done is to do it immediately. Do it now. Do it the moment it comes up. It's amazing how much time can be lost by picking up a task, looking at it, starting it, then putting it down and coming back to it again and again. Sometimes small tasks should be done as fast as they arise. This will get you a reputation for being the kind of person to give jobs to when you want them done quickly. Successful people are those who have developed the habits of success. Fully 95 percent of everything you do throughout your day is based on habit. Successful people form good habits and allow those habits to govern their behaviors. Unsuccessful people allow bad habits to form, and these bad habits can then lead to frustration and failure.

My friend Ed Foreman says, good habits are hard to form but easy to live with. Bad habits, on the other hand, are easy to form but hard to live with. What kind of habits do you have?

You develop a habit by repetition. You do the same thing over and over again until it becomes automatic. Successful people have developed automatic success habits. They have trained themselves like athletes to do certain things in a certain way over and over again so that they do them automatically without their even thinking about them.

One habit of success is that of early rising. Successful people get up a little bit earlier, read and get ready, plan, organize their day on paper, and get going before the average person even gets started. I met a woman recently who found that by getting up at four o'clock in the morning, she could do the equivalent of a full day's work by seven or eight o'clock—before the average person even got into gear. In no time at all, she was earning double the amount of her coworkers. She was continually promoted, advanced, and paid more money because she was getting far more done than anyone else. She was adding far more value.

Successful people make a habit of getting up earlier, usually by six or 6:30 in the morning and then getting going immediately. Average people, on the other hand, takes a full hour to get up, get going, and drag themselves off to work, but this is definitely not for you. When your alarm clock goes off, get up immediately, and get going right away. Start moving.

Also, make a habit of punctuality.

Be on time or, better yet, early for every appointment. Get into work before anyone else, and when you arrive, begin working immediately. Don't waste time in reading the newspaper, drinking coffee, or idly socializing. Develop a reputation for being the kind of person who is always working on high-priority tasks. Work all the time you work. Discipline yourself to keep yourself focused continually. Don't allow other people to put you off your game. When you have coffee breaks or lunches, have them when they best suit you, not when they best suit the clock. Make a habit of working a little bit later than the average person.

Here's a powerful formula that you can use to double your productivity (and maybe even your income) over the next twelve months. It's very simple and it works for anyone who uses it.

First, come into work one hour earlier. This doesn't take very much effort and it allows you to beat the traffic. When you get in, have your work all planned, and then put your head down and go full blast. Statistics show that you can do three hours of work in one hour of uninterrupted time in the office. If you're in sales, schedule your first appointment as early as possible. Many of the most important people you could want to see get into the office at 7 or 7:30 in the morning, so arrange to meet them there. One salesman friend of mine, who was at the top of his field, found that the key to getting appointments with the key decision-makers was to call their offices at 7 in the morning or 6:30 or 7 in the evening. He found that at these times, all the staff had either gone home or weren't in yet. The only people still working were the key people. They would answer the phone personally, and he would get an opportunity to talk to them and arrange to see them later.

Develop the habit of moving fast.

Develop the habit of moving fast. As I said before, fast trackers in every field have a sense of urgency. Only a small percentage of the population moves quickly when opportunity or responsibility presents itself. You must be a member of this small percentage. When I was younger, I used to think that when my opportunity came along, I would take advantage of it at that time. I soon learned that your opportunity never does just come along. The key to this truth is contained in the story called "Acres of Diamonds" by Russell Conwell. In short, it says that your greatest opportunities lie under your own feet. They are right where you are. They lie within your current talents, skills, ability, and experience. They lie within your own business or industry. They lie within your own background or career. Your acres of diamonds are under your own feet, and that is where you should start to look.

Theodore Roosevelt once said, "Do what you can with what you have right where you are"; this is the key to success. Focus on the present moment and your current situation. Don't wait for things to be just right. It is you who will make things just right by throwing your whole heart into what you're doing right now every minute. You'll open up doors of opportunity that are not now even visible to you. Look around you at this very moment and ask yourself, what could I do to add value for the most important people in my work life? What could you do to make things faster, easier, or better for the people who depend on you? Be proactive rather than reactive. Be the kind of person who reaches out and grabs opportunities; if you don't have any opportunities, create them through your own efforts.

Many years ago, a secretary in Boca Raton, Florida, told me an interesting story at one of my seminars. She had listened to one of my audio programs and set a goal to increase her income by 50 percent in the next year. But she felt it was probably impossible in her company, because she was part of a large secretarial pool, and salaries were pretty much fixed. Everyone made more or less the same. Nonetheless, she decided to look for ways to add value for her boss. She noticed that he spent a lot of time replying to correspondence. She began replying to the correspondence for him and taking the finished letters to him to edit and sign. Soon she had taken over the responsibility of handling 90 percent of his regular correspondence.

In addition, she began to take additional courses to upgrade her skills in word processing, page making, and report preparation. Bit by bit, she began to take smaller tasks away from him and do them eventually in an excellent fashion. After about three months, her boss called her in and closed the door. He said to her that he really appreciated the things that she was doing for him and he wanted to increase her pay. He asked her not to tell anyone else so that it didn't make any waves around the office, but he raised her salary from $1,500 to $1,750 per month. She continued looking for ways to add value to his work. Three months later, he increased her pay again and three months later, again, until by the end of the year, she was making $2,250 per month while the other secretaries around her was still earning an average of $1,500. She was amazed at what happened when she set a goal and began to focus all of her energies on adding value for her boss and her company, and this same strategy can work for you.

Every job is an opportunity for you to solve problems and to satisfy the needs of other people. The problems and needs that people have are unlimited; the opportunities for you to create value are unlimited as well. Every fortune begins with an idea to serve people better in some way. Entrepreneurs who start and build a successful company have usually worked successfully for another organization, where they continually looked for ways to increase their value to the company.

Again, the primary sources of value, the keys to wealth building, are time and knowledge. Your job is to continually increase your knowledge so that the value of what you do becomes greater and greater. You've heard it said that knowledge is power, but this is only partially true. It is only knowledge that can be applied to some good purpose that is power. Your job is to gather the knowledge that you need so that you can do your job fast and well.

There's a saying in Texas: "It's not the size of the dog in the fight, it's the size of the fight in the dog." Your ability to contribute value to your current situation, either as an employee or as an employer, as a company worker or company owner, will determine your income and your financial future.

Successful people are more productive than unsuccessful people. They have better habits. They dream bigger dreams, they work from written goals, they do what they love to do, and they concentrate on getting better and better at it. They use their natural abilities to the full. They're continually generating ideas to solve problems and move ahead. They focus on applying themselves for maximum results. Above all, they're constantly looking around for opportunities to add value to everything they do. They have a sense of urgency and a bias for action. They work all the time they work. They develop a tremendous sense of forward momentum. They soon begin to feel unstoppable, and so will you.

Key Points in This Chapter

1. The law of cause and effect: for every effect, there are specific causes. Everything happens for a reason.
2. The reality principle: you must deal with the world as it is, not as you wish it would be.
3. Fully 50 percent of all working time is wasted.
4. The forty-plus formula: every hour that you put in over forty hours on your job or on yourself is an investment in your future.
5. All wealth comes from adding value.
6. There are two major sources of value today: time and knowledge.
7. The most important quality that you can develop with regard to time is a sense of urgency.
8. All success is based on habit.

six

The Power of Decision

Successful people are not necessarily those who make the right decisions, but they make their decisions right. They think it through, make a decision, take action, get feedback, self-correct, and continue on.

In a recent study, several managers were divided into two groups: those who were on the fast track in their careers and moving ahead rapidly, and those who had flattened out and seemed to be going nowhere. They gave both groups of managers the same set of written decision-making tests. Both groups of managers scored equally well: they were both equally competent in their ability to analyze the situation and make the correct decision on paper.

What accounted for the success of one group of managers versus the others? It was simply this: the successful group actually made the decisions and took action after thinking, while the second group of managers was fearful and indecisive and afraid to make a decision in the real world for fear that it would turn out poorly.

> The greatest obstacle to success is fear.

As I've already emphasized, the greatest obstacle to success—the common denominator of learned helplessness and the comfort zone—is fear of all kinds, especially the fear of failure. The fear of failure does more to hold you back than anything else It makes people indecisive and vacillating. It causes people to hesitate and procrastinate. The fear of failure, the fear that they might make a mistake, causes people to sabotage themselves and their careers year after year.

Successful people are decisive. They have developed the habit of considering the information carefully and then taking action. Even though there's no certainty about the outcome, they're likely to learn ways of making better choices.

The ideas and methods that I'm about to discuss have been developed and applied by the most successful men and women in our society. Once you have these mental tools, you can use them for the rest of your life.

The Seven-Step Method

Here is a seven-step method that will help you solve more problems and make better decisions. It is simple and powerful. It contains the basic elements of problem-solving and decision-making that you can apply to any area of your life.

1. Approach the problem or difficulty confidently and optimistically. Instead of calling it a *problem*, call it a *situation*. *Problem* is a

> ### The Seven-Step Method
> 1. Approach the problem or difficulty confidently and optimistically.
> 2. Define your situation clearly.
> 3. Ask, what are all the possible causes of this problem?
> 4. Define all the possible solutions.
> 5. Make a decision.
> 6. Assign responsibility for carrying out the decision.
> 7. Set a deadline.

negative word, while *situation* is a neutral word. In one well-known example, at the beginning of each year, the chairman of the company would enter the meeting room with a brand-new dictionary and a pair of scissors. With great fanfare, he would open the dictionary to the word *problem*, cut it out with the scissors, and burn the paper in an ashtray. He would then say, "Ladies and gentlemen, we have many situations in this company, but we have no problems. We don't use the word *problem* around here. A better word is the word *challenge*." A situation is neutral, but a challenge is something that you rise to, something that brings out the very best in you. Even better is the word *opportunity*. An opportunity enables you to take advantage of the details or factors in a situation. Everyone is looking for opportunities, and within every problem is contained the seeds of an equal or greater opportunity or benefit. Your job is to find it.

2. Define your situation clearly. What exactly is the situation? What are you worrying about? A primary reason for worry over

difficulties is the failure to define them clearly. Look for ways to expand or improve your definition of the problem situation. For example, once you define it clearly in writing, you can ask yourself, what else is the problem?

When I consult with marketing organizations, they might say their problem is that their sales are not high enough. If your sales aren't high enough, that would dictate a particular line of thinking and a particular set of possible solutions.

But what if you redefined the problem and said instead that your customers are not buying enough from you? This is a different statement of the same problem, but it leads you in a different direction for solutions. If your customers are not buying enough, what could you do to induce them to buy more?

How could you present your product or service in a more appealing way so that more customers would be more likely to consume it?

Another definition of the same problem is that your customers are buying too much of your product or service from your competitors. This leads you in another different direction. What do your prospective customers see in your competitors' offerings? How could you offset the perceived advantages that your customers find in your competitors?

Perhaps the best way of redefining this problem situation is to say that your salespeople are not selling enough of your products or services to prospective customers. This would lead you in the direction of improved sales and management training, different methods of supervision, and field management.In every case, stating and restating the problem in a variety of different ways can lead you to totally different approaches to solving it and make it much more likely that you will come up with a good decision.

3. Ask, what are all the possible causes of this particular problem situation? People tend to think there are only one or two solutions and then choose among them, but the quantity of possible solutions that you can develop (as in brainstorming) determines the quality of the one that you finally settle upon.

At this stage of the process, your job is to develop as many different, even ridiculous, solutions as possible. One approach that has always helped me in dealing with any difficult situation is to imagine for a moment that everything that I am doing right now is dead wrong. This exercise opens my mind to far more possibilities than if I assume that the solution lies in doing what I'm currently doing in a slightly different way. What if you were completely wrong in the most difficult situation that you are currently facing? What if the correct answer was exactly the opposite of what you're committed to doing right now? How would this change your approach?

4. Define all the possible solutions based on your definition of the problem and the possible reasons for it. Write down as many different solutions as you can find; use brainstorming and/or mindstorming if suitable. The more different solutions and combinations of solutions that you can come up with, the better decision you will make at the end.

> Often any decision is better than no decision.

5. Once you've developed a variety of solutions, make a decision. Often any decision is better than no decision. Fully 80 percent of

problem situations that you face should be dealt with and solved immediately. Indecisiveness and procrastination on minor decisions is a major source of stress and a terrible time waster.

Before you take action, ask yourself these two questions: first, what is the worst possible thing that can happen if you implement this solution? Think of the ultimate downside. Fill out the disaster report on this particular solution. The late J. Paul Getty, the world's richest man at one time, said that one of his secrets for success before entering into any business deal was to determine the worst possible thing that could happen if it went wrong. He said the second part was to make sure that that didn't happen.

The second question you ask before you implement your decision is, what else is the solution? Your ability to develop a plan B—an alternate solution to keep in your back pocket in case the first solution doesn't work—gives you tremendous flexibility. The most successful leaders throughout human history have been flexible thinkers in that they have always had alternatives completely developed and ready to go in case their first decision didn't work out.

6. Assign specific responsibility for carrying out the decision. Who exactly is going to take the actions necessary? What exactly is to be done? If several people are involved, what are the exact, specific responsibilities of each person? Many decisions fall apart because no one was assigned the specific responsibility for carrying them out.

> A decision without a deadline is merely a verbal exercise.

7. Set a deadline. If it's a major decision, set subdeadlines and schedules for checking on progress. A decision without a deadline is a conversation without an end; it is merely a verbal exercise. A deadline locks in the decision and makes it something hard and tangible that people can relate to and act upon.

The Genius of Boldness

Once you've made a decision, never consider the possibility of failure. As I said earlier, it is the fear of failure that holds people back rather than failure itself. The power of decision—your willingness to make clear, unequivocal decisions and take action in the direction of your goals—will eventually make everything possible for you.

There is a passage often attributed to the great German poet Johann Wolfgang von Goethe, although it actually appears in a book by a Scottish explorer named William Hutchinson Murray. Nevertheless, it remains powerful:

> Until one is committed, there is hesitancy, the chance to draw back—concerning all acts of initiative (and creation), there is one elementary truth that ignorance of which kills countless ideas and splendid plans: that the moment one definitely commits oneself, then Providence moves too. All sorts of things occur to help one that would never otherwise have occurred. A whole stream of events issues from the decision, raising in one's favor all manner of unforeseen incidents and meetings and material assistance, which no man could have dreamed would have come his way.
>
> Whatever you can do, or dream you can do, begin it. Boldness has genius, power, and magic in it. Begin it now.

Decision activates your mental powers.

Decision activates your mental powers. It increases your courage and confidence and raises your self-esteem. It boosts your energy and enthusiasm and raises your level of self-expectancy. Making clear, unequivocal decisions about who you are, what you want to accomplish, and what you're going to do frees you of the indecisiveness that traps most people. Don't be afraid of failing occasionally; all great successes were once great failures.

Thomas Edison was perhaps the greatest failure in the history of invention, but he was also the most successful inventor of the modern age. By 1930, fully one sixth of the American working population was employed producing products invented by Edison.

His attitude toward his experiments was very instructive. He kept excellent notes on every experiment. He was certain that he would find the solution he was looking for if he kept on long enough. Each time an experiment failed, he looked upon it as having successfully identified one more way that did not work. In his own mind, that put him one experiment closer to what he was looking for. He made over 11,000 experiments before he discovered the carbon-impregnated filament that led to the first electric light bulb, but he never wavered. For him, success was a process of eliminating all the ways that didn't work until there was only one way left.

Today, we live in the information age. Its foundation is the computer and the software programs that run in those computers. A software program is made up of many hundreds of thousands and millions of lines of code. Software programmers often spend many months designing the binary codes that allow a program to run smoothly. But do you think that even the most sophisticated software program, developed by the most sophisticated software engineers, works right the first time? Of course not. When a program is ready for its first run, the designers know that it's full of bugs. They know that it is a natural part of the process of software development to begin running the program and removing the bugs one by one.

Many developers put their new, untried software onto the Internet and offer it at no charge to anyone who wants to pick it up. Those who pick up the software and download it into their computers go to work. In no time at all, they begin to find the bugs that have not yet been removed and report them back to the troubleshooting division of the software developer. The developer then incorporates those comments into the ongoing redesign of the program until it works perfectly. But the developer knows that if you remove the bugs one after another as they are discovered, eventually the program will be nearly flawless and can then be multiplied thousands or millions of times and sold all over the world.

Your life is much the same.

When you start off as a young person, there are a lot of bugs in your program. Your job is to continue learning, have an experience, evaluating the experience and removing the bugs until you get smarter and smarter.

You are a learning organism.

You are a learning organism. You are learning at a fantastic rate. In the first two years of your life, you learn to coordinate twenty-six different senses. You learn to walk, talk, interact, and develop a social personality. You learn how to control your body, emotions, face, and hearing. You learn how to coordinate sounds, smells, taste, sensations, and images. You learn at such a phenomenal rate that you'll probably never learn again at the same speed, but even as an adult, you still learn at an incredible rate. With everything that you do, you act like a cybernetic mechanism, constantly taking feedback from your environment, incorporating it into your knowledge base, and adjusting your course accordingly. The more information you take in and the more different things you try, the faster you learn, the smarter you get, and the more rapidly you move ahead. A high degree of failure ensures a high degree of success.

The author Arthur Gordon once approached Thomas J. Watson Sr., the founder of IBM, and asked him how he could be more successful as a writer faster. Watson replied with these profound words: "If you want to be successful faster, you must double your rate of failure. Success lies on the far side of failure." The more you have already failed in life, the more likely you are to be on the verge of great successes. In a multiyear study of luck and good fortune, one researcher found that a streak of good luck seems to follow a streak of bad luck. It is all a matter of probabilities. The more you try, the more you triumph.

The Dynamic of Priorities

One of the most important elements of decisiveness is your ability to choose among priorities: to look at all the different things you could do and the directions that you can go in and decide among them correctly. In fact, your ability to make the right choices and decisions will determine everything that happens to you. A successful life is the result of a series of successful choices and decisions. An unsuccessful life is the result of a series of poor choices and decisions.

In his book *Yes or No*, Spencer Johnson says the starting point of making better decisions is to stop making worse decisions. The starting point of moving ahead rapidly is often to stop doing the things that are holding you back.

> The worst use of your time is to do very well what need not be done at all.

There are some very important rules regarding priorities. The first is that the worst use of your time is to do well what need not be done at all. Many people spend an enormous amount of time in needless perfectionism. They work for hours getting a particular job or task exactly right when it is not even important in the first place. Often they do this unconsciously, because it enables them to avoid coming to grips with the really important tasks and responsibilities, where big differences can be made and big failures are possible.

The fear of failure is insidious. It sits deep down in your subconscious mind and sabotages you without your even knowing it. One manifestation of the fear of failure is the tendency to procrastinate when faced with large tasks or multiple responsibilities. The average person continually puts off doing the things that, if they did them and did them well, would make the greatest difference in their lives. Don't let this happen to you.

Another rule with regard to priorities is that since you can only do one thing at a time, choosing to do one thing means simultaneously choosing not to do everything else for that moment.

Sometimes it is useful to think about what you will *not* be doing before you start on a particular action. Turning on the television at night means not spending time talking to your spouse or your children. Reading the newspaper or socializing in the office means not getting on with the important tasks that are essential to your success.

The third point about setting priorities is that every action or inaction is a choice between what is more valuable and what is less valuable. Your ability to choose among competing alternatives determines everything that happens to you. It's essential to learn to choose well.

Work from a List

One of the most useful tools for making better choices and setting better priorities is a list. Make a list before you start work, preferably the night before. Always work from a list. Think on paper. Highly productive people write everything down before they begin. Then go over your written list, and set priorities for each item. As a general rule, the planning and preparation you put into a task before you begin has the greatest impact on the final result. You've heard it said: well begun is half done.

The key mental tool for evaluating your work before you begin is the consideration of future consequences, either positive or negative. With every action, there are consequences, secondary consequences, and unexpected consequences. Your ability to think through each of these will have as much impact on your success as any other factor. The highly productive person is extremely accurate in predicting what might happen as the result of a certain course of action.

The immediate, obvious consequences are what should materialize as a result of cause and effect. Every action you take is aimed at an improvement of some kind: a consequence that would not occur if you didn't do something. As a result, immediately expected consequences are always positive and aimed at a betterment of your conditions. Otherwise you would not take that action.

Secondary consequences, however, can be even more important. These things are likely to happen afterwards as a result of what you do to achieve the primary consequences. These secondary consequences, and your ability to identify them accurately, can have an enormous positive or negative impact on the final result.

Here's a simple example. A person has a few drinks with friends, stays longer than he expected, and sets out to drive home in a hurry under the influence of alcohol. The initial drinks and socializing plus the extra time were aimed at achieving the positive consequences of a pleasant social evening.

What are the secondary consequences?

The driver is now in a hurry to get home at night, drunk. If he has an accident and hurts himself or someone else, the secondary consequences of drinking too much and staying too late can be disastrous.

Here's another example. A young person wastes his time in high school, barely graduates, gets a low-paid job, and spends his evening socializing or watching television. What are the likely consequences of this lifestyle and these choices? Probably a lifetime of poorly paid work, limited promotion and opportunities, a substandard lifestyle, constant worry about money, limited freedom, an unexciting social circle, and an eventual sense of hopelessness and despair. It was fun to get out of school, get an easy job, and have a good time, but the secondary consequences are unhappiness and failure.

Unexpected consequences can cause you to end up far worse off than if you had never initiated the action at all.

Parents who give their children everything they ask for in an attempt to make them happy in the short term often end up creating uncontrollable, spoiled, selfish children who resent their parents and doubt themselves.

> Short-term gain often leads to long-term pain.
> Short-term pain often leads to long-term gain.

With potential consequences, short-term gain often leads to long-term pain. The opposite is true as well: short-term pain often leads to long-term gain. Always think of the difficult, disciplined, determined things you can do today that will lead to greater riches, rewards, and satisfactions in the future. Think long-term, not short-term. Play down the board in your life. Think about the future. The decisions that you make about long-term consequences will determine the quality of your entire life.

Setting Posteriorities

Developing the power of decision also requires setting posteriorities. A priority is something that you do more of and sooner. A posteriority is something that you do less of and later, if at all. The only way that you can get more time to do more of the things that make a difference in your life is by deciding what activities you are going to cut back on or discontinue. As you grow through life, one of your most important decisions is determining the activities and social functions that you are no longer going to engage in. You need to remove these time-wasting, time-consuming activities from your life in order to have enough time to do the things that are really important to you.

Another tool that you can use to be more decisive is the 80/20 rule, which we've already encountered. This simply says that 80 percent of your results come from 20 percent of what you do: 80 percent of your sales come from 20 percent of your customers, 80 percent of your profits come from 20 percent of your products, and so on.

Before beginning any set of tasks, stand back and determine which 20 percent of them will account for 80 percent of your results. Then discipline yourself to go to work on those key tasks, and stay with them until they're done.

Concentration

This brings us to perhaps the most important single principle in decisiveness: the principle of concentration. Learning to concentrate is one of the most important tasks of adult life. It's never easy, but with it, you can do almost anything; without it, you can do almost nothing.

Here's a simple formula. You've gone through all the previous exercises of making decisions and setting priorities. Your job now is to select the single most important thing that you could possibly be doing. You ask yourself: "If I were to be called out of town for a month and I could only complete one task before I left, what task would that be?"

This question will help you to clear your mind completely. You'll see that one of the biggest and most difficult tasks on your plate is probably the one that could make the greatest difference in your life if you were to get it done and done well. You then decide to concentrate single-mindedly on this task and stay at it until it's done. Persevere without diversion or distraction. Focus all of your mind and energies on getting this job finished, no matter how long it takes.

In his book *The Time Trap*, Alex Mackenzie talks about one of the most important principles of time management ever discovered: *single handling*. It consists of selecting your most important task and staying with it until it's 100 percent complete.

> Select your most important task and stay with it until it's 100 percent complete.

The principle of concentration, combined with single handling, will enable you to accomplish extraordinary things. The inability to select the biggest and most important task in front of you and discipline yourself to stay with it until it's complete is a primary reason for failure in adult life.

In the simplest terms, successful people spend more time doing more productive things. Failures spend more time doing less productive things. The primary difference between success and failure is time usage versus time wastage.

Successful people take a lot of time to think about where they are and where they want to go. They use personal strategic planning to chart their course and to analyze each step. They focus their energies and attention on the one or two things they can do that can make the greatest difference in their lives. They concentrate single-mindedly on those things, and they discipline themselves to stay at them until they're successfully completed. They're highly productive in everything they do.

Unsuccessful people, on the other hand, do many things that have little or no value. They often consume their entire day clearing up small details, warming up, and getting ready for the one or two big tasks that really count. By the time they have cleared up their small tasks, the day is gone. They feel stressed and anxious and go home fatigued, talking about what a tough day they have had. They are stressed primarily because their major tasks are building up like an avalanche overhang about to come down on them. Your big tasks don't go away if they don't get done; they just sit there waiting and accumulating with others.

Keep asking yourself, what is the most valuable use of my time right now? Every hour of every day, stop yourself and ask, is this the most valuable use of my time? Is this the most important thing that I could possibly be doing at this moment? The power of decision comes from clarity: you become more decisive when you organize your plans and your work and set clear priorities on what you have to do. You become more decisive when you resolve to overcome the fears of failure and act even though there's no guarantee of success.

Decisiveness activates your positive mind and releases your creativity. If you make a habit of being decisive—a habit possessed by the most successful and effective people—you will become more powerful, more positive, more confident, and more creative. You will shift from positive thinking to positive knowing. You will develop a deep sense of control, confidence, and courage that will enable you to move forward even against overwhelming odds.

Key Points in This Chapter

1. The greatest obstacle to success is fear.
2. Successful people are decisive.
3. Use the seven-step method for solving problems.
4. Once you've made a decision, set a deadline for carrying it out.
5. You learn at an incredible rate all your life.
6. Set priorities and posteriorities.
7. Work from a list.
8. Select your most important task, and stay with it until it's 100 percent complete.

seven

Possibility Thinking

The way you think about yourself and your life determines almost everything that happens to you. Your primary business must be to take full control over your thinking and keep your words and thoughts clearly focused on what you want in life. You must also keep your words and thoughts free from the things that you *don't* want. This simple formula is the real key to success, achievement, happiness, and personal growth.

In this chapter, I'm going to talk about possibility thinking. With possibility thinking, you continually look at your world and the events around you in terms of possibilities rather than difficulties or problems. This is a habitual way of thinking, and, like all habits, it is learned. You can develop it with constant repetition until you become a positive and constructive person.

A positive mental attitude, which is closely associated with success, has been talked about for many years. We know that the kind of people that we like and want to be around tend to be those who are generally cheerful about themselves and their activities. No one wants to be around a negative, pessimistic, complaining person.

Unfortunately, it's easy to slip into the habit of complaining and seeing things negatively. We are surrounded by negative influences on radio, television, newspapers, magazines, and, unfortunately, in our daily associations with others. It's hard to rise above the flood of negativity that engulfs us, but it's absolutely essential if you want to keep your spirits up and achieve your goals.

A positive mental attitude can be defined as *a constructive response to stress.*

A positive mental attitude can be defined as *a constructive response to stress.* Stress is inevitable. Failures, disappointments, setbacks, obstacles, and difficulties occur to everyone all the time.

The only thing over which you have any control is how you respond to these events.

If you respond in a positive, constructive way, you'll maintain a positive attitude. As a result, you'll be more creative and alert and more likely to see opportunities to solve your problems and move toward accomplishing your goals. If you respond negatively, your response will shut down certain parts of your brain. You'll be less and less creative. You'll be more and more likely to react instinctively and in a negative way.

The Five-Step Power Process

There is a five-step power process that you can learn to practice and accelerate goal attainment and to keep yourself positive most of the time. This five-step process condenses the best that we've learned in behavioral psychology. It contains and illustrates all of the key principles that you need to know to be a highly effective, positive, possibility thinker.

The five steps are: (1) idealize, (2) verbalize, (3) visualize, (4) emotionalize, and (5) realize. Let me go through them one by one.

The Five-Step Process

1. Idealize
2. Verbalize
3. Visualize
4. Emotionalize
5. Realize

Idealize

The starting point of changing your life and your personality, raising your self-esteem, and improving your levels of self-confidence and courage is to begin to idealize the kind of life that you want to have a week, a month, a year, and even five years from now. In chapter 1, I talked about dreaming big dreams. In idealizing, you go through each of the key areas of your life and imagine what it would look like if every part of it were exactly as you would want it to be, in every respect.

Start with your income. How much do you want to be earning one, two, three, and five years from today? What knowledge, skills, and abilities will you need to earn that amount? What kind of work will you be doing? What level will you have to be at in your company or profession? Whom will you have to be selling to, and what kinds of products and services will you have to be offering?

When you idealize your income and your lifestyle, you begin to become a visionary in your own life. You begin to practice the most important quality of personal leadership: projecting into the future and thinking about how you can make your future dreams a current reality.

Always begin with a mission statement of exactly how you want to be sometime in the future.

When doing personal strategic planning, you always begin with a mission statement: a statement of exactly how you want to be sometime in the future. You could say, "I am a healthy, happy, positive personality who does excellent work, is paid extremely well, and is highly respected by his coworkers and deeply loved by his family." This mission statement serves as an organizing principle that you can use to compare against what you are doing right now on a day-to-day basis to see if it's consistent with where you want to end up.

I once conducted a strategic planning session for a large corporation. They had more than 250 potential projects on their plate. After we had defined the values, vision, and ideal mission of the company, they were immediately able to discard more than 200 of those projects. It was clear to everyone at the meeting that these projects were not consistent with who they were and where they wanted to be in the future.

This can work for you as well. One of your problems is that you are overwhelmed with too much to do, too many things to think about, too many possibilities, and too little time. By becoming clear about where you want to end up in the future, you can begin creatively abandoning things that are simply not consistent with your highest good.

You should idealize your health as well.

Exactly how much do you want to weigh, and what level of fitness do you want to enjoy? How does that compare with where you are today? What steps will you have to take, and what changes will you have to make in your health habits in order to become the ideal person that you desire to be physically? This becomes your future vision for yourself, your ideal.

You should also idealize with regard to your family relationships. A good friend of mine sat down with his wife and children not long ago, and they idealized together about how to best spend their time as a family if they had no limitations. As a result of this exercise, they made some decisions. They moved out of the big city to a larger home with a bigger yard in the country. He reorganized his work week so that he worked ten- and twelve-hour days, four days per week, in the city, and three or four hours per day in his home office in the country.

He ended up spending far more time with his family and getting far more satisfaction out of life. Moreover, both his results and his income increased with his new plan.

What kind of a person do you want to be in the future?

Set ideals with regard to your personal and professional development. What kind of a person do you want to be in the future?

What kind of additional knowledge and skills do you want to acquire? Do you want to learn languages or become fluent with computers and online services? What subjects do you want to explore? What is your growth plan to get from where you are to where you want to go?

Defining your ideal in any important area of your life is the starting point of making present decisions that will lead to greater success and happiness in the future. As you move towards the achievement of a worthy ideal, you feel happier and more confident.

The more progress you make toward a clear goal or set of ideal conditions, the more energy and enthusiasm you have.

Intelligence is doing things that move you in the direction of your highest goals.

In a study of highly successful men and women by the Gallup Organization, respondents attributed much of their success to intelligence. But when the pollsters asked the subjects to define intelligence, they got a very interesting answer: they defined intelligence as a way of acting, as doing only those things that move them in the direction of their highest goals and ambitions. They further defined intelligence as thinking through and eliminating time-consuming activities that did not move them in the direction of their goals or moved them away from their goals. Whenever you are doing something that's moving you in the direction of your own goals and ideals, you are acting intelligently. This is true regardless of your education or IQ.

This is why many people of supposedly average intelligence are accomplishing far more than people with university degrees: the former are focusing their time and activities on accomplishing only the goals that are uppermost in their minds and hearts.

Verbalize

The second part of this five-step process is to clearly verbalize the things that you want to do, have, and be. By verbalization, I mean the use of positive affirmations. With them, your potential is unlimited.

The law of subconscious activity says that whatever you repeat over and over to yourself in your conscious mind will eventually be accepted by your subconscious mind. Once your subconscious mind accepts your conscious thoughts as a command, it goes to work to bring those goals into your life. With positive affirmations, you can take full control over the programming of your subconscious mind. You can tap into an enormous power that can help you twenty-four hours per day to move toward higher income, better health, better relationships, and greater success.

> A positive affirmation is *personal*, *positive*, and *present-tense*.

A positive affirmation is based on the three Ps: it is *personal*, *positive*, and *present-tense*. Your subconscious mind can only take in new information that is framed in positive, personal, present-tense form.

One of the best affirmations is, "I like myself." Repeat it over and over again. When you repeat the words, "I like myself" over and over dozens of times per day, you drive this message deep into your subconscious mind. This affirmation raises your self-esteem, and your performance improves in everything that you attempt. The more you like yourself, the better you do, and the better you do, the more you like yourself.

Another great affirmation that you can use continually is to repeat the words, "I'm the best." By continually talking to yourself in highly positive terms and being your own cheerleader, you find yourself doing better and better at everything you attempt.

Another wonderful affirmation, which I began using many years ago is, "I love my work." Sometimes when you wake up in the morning, you don't feel particularly excited about your work, but you can take control over your mental processes by repeating, "I love my work" until it feels true.

One of the very best affirmations is to say, "I like myself, and I love my work." This affirmation, repeated enthusiastically several times every morning, will rev you up and get you excited about going to your job.

Ninety-five percent of your emotions are determined by the way you talk to yourself. Dr. Martin Seligman's work on learned optimism at the University of Pennsylvania concluded that your explanatory style is the critical factor in determining whether you are a positive or negative person. Your explanatory style is defined as how you explain things to yourself. If you explain things to yourself in a positive way, you tend to be positive. If you explain them in a negative way, you tend to be negative. Seligman concluded that optimistic people, when something goes wrong, explain it as though it were a temporary, specific situation rather than a long-term general condition. Say you make a sales call, and it doesn't work out. If you're a positive person, you'll say something like, "Well, it's just one sales call." This makes it temporary.

You'll say, "The customer's probably having a bad day." This makes it specific. You say," I'll be more successful on the next call." This makes you future-oriented. When you dismiss temporary setbacks in this way, you remain a pretty cheerful person.

Negative people, on the other hand, interpret a problem as a statement about their personal deficiencies. If the sales call doesn't work out, they say, "I must be a terrible salesperson. The product's no good. Customers aren't interested in what we have to sell," or "I'll never succeed in this field." They overgeneralize and overdramatize a small failure rather than dismissing it and going on to the next call.

This is purely a matter of choice. You control your emotions by how you choose to explain a situation to yourself.

> You control your emotions by how you choose to explain a situation to yourself.

In verbalizing your goals through positive affirmations, you should use words that your subconscious can relate to easily. Make your statements simple and practical. "I like myself" is personal. "I'm the best" is personal and positive, and "I love my work" is personal, positive and present-tense. In each case, these affirmations are immediately accepted by your subconscious mind as commands, and they immediately have an impact on how you think and feel about yourself.

You can keep yourself positive and optimistic by continually talking to yourself in positive ways. Sometimes this is called your *interpretive style*: how you interpret things that are happening around you. The multimillionaire W. Clement Stone was famous for being an "inverse paranoid." A paranoid is someone who believes that people are conspiring against him or her. An inverse paranoid, on the other hand, is a person who is convinced that the world is conspiring to make him successful. He looks upon everything that happens as part of a great plan with a positive meaning.

Stone used to respond to every difficulty with the emphatic statement, "That's good," and he would go to work to find out what was good about the situation.

Remember when I talked about the power of decision? I said that if you change the definition of a problem to that of a situation, a challenge, or, even better, an opportunity, your response to it will be completely different. If you look at every problem as a potential opportunity, you'll often find within it an opportunity that you can use. The late inspirational author Norman Vincent Peale used to say that when God wants to send you a gift, he wraps it up in a problem. The bigger the problem, the bigger the gift in the form of valuable lessons, ideas, and insights that it probably contains. Is the glass half full or is it half empty? It's up to you.

Visualize

The third part of the five-point process is visualization. I've talked about visualization before and how powerful it is in helping you to achieve your goals. (By the way, everyone visualizes, but successful people visualize the things they want, and unsuccessful people visualize the things they don't want.)

Let me give you a simple example. Prior to every new experience, successful people recall and relive a previous successful experience of that same kind. Unsuccessful people, prior to a new experience, recall and relive a previous failure. In either way, they're creating a predisposition and instruction to their subconscious mind to act in a manner consistent with their visualization.

In visualizing, you project your mind forward, and you soak your mind in a picture of your ideal future goal. You imagine what it would look like if it were already achieved. You make your picture as vivid as possible. You repeat this mental picture over and over as often as you possibly can during the day and for as long a time as you can.

There's a direct relationship between how clearly you visualize on the inside and how rapidly your goal comes into reality on the outside. Visualization is one of the most powerful faculties that can enable you to become a possibility thinker, to think big about your life and your future, and to make your current dreams into future realities.

You can use three techniques that combine verbalization and visualization. These are often called *mental programming techniques*, and they're extraordinarily effective in preparing yourself mentally for an upcoming event.

The first method is the *quick programming technique*. Prior to any nonrecurring event of importance, like a sales call, a meeting, or an interview, take a few moments and prepare your mind.

Take a few deep breaths, which drops your mind into the alpha state and makes your subconscious mind receptive to an incoming command. You then visualize the ideal outcome of the situation you are going into. For example, if you're making a sales call, visualize the client responding to you in a happy, positive way. Especially visualize the client signing the check or sales order at the end of the conversation. One of my good friends has used this for many years to become one of the highest-paid people in his industry. He says it is absolutely amazing how many times the sales situation works out exactly as he visualized it before he went in. Try it for yourself and see.

The next part of the quick programming technique is to verbalize or create a positive affirmation that is consistent with your mental picture. A simple affirmation would be something like, "This sales call goes extremely well and concludes satisfactorily for everyone involved." This simply instructs your subconscious mind to give you the words, feelings, actions, reactions, and body language consistent with achieving your goal of a successful call.

We teach this same quick affirmation technique to people going on job interviews, people giving public talks, people performing in the arts, and even to politicians. It's an extraordinarily effective technique, and it only takes a few seconds prior to each event.

The second way to keep yourself positive and focused is the *standard affirmation technique.* This involves writing out your major goals in the form of present, positive, personal affirmations on three by five index cards, one goal per card. Carry these cards around with you. At the beginning of each day, take a few minutes by yourself and read through your cards. You can work on ten to fifteen goals at a time using this method.

Take the first card and read it. Perhaps the first card says, "I earn $250,000 per year." This is positive, personal, and present-tense. Read the card, and let your eyes focus on the message so that it transfers into your subconscious mind. Then close your eyes. Take a deep breath and repeat the affirmation five times. As you affirm, visualize your goal as already achieved; see it, feel it. Then open your eyes and read the next card.

> As you affirm, visualize your goal as
> already achieved; see it, feel it.

This entire exercise with ten or fifteen goals takes about ten minutes. It programs your entire subconscious mind and prepares you to perform at your best for the rest of the day for attaining each of your goals. If you do this each morning and each evening before you start out and before you go to bed, you'll be amazed at how quickly your goals begin to materialize. Someone once said, "I'd rather begin a day without breakfast than begin a day without affirmations."

By the way, your subconscious mind controls the power of attraction in your life, so the more you feed your subconscious mind with words and pictures that consistent with what you want to accomplish, the more you become a living magnet and attract people, opportunities, ideas, and resources that make your goals a possibility.

The third programming technique that you can use is often called *mental rehearsal*. In sports psychology, you sit or lie down completely relaxed, with your eyes closed, and breathe deeply until your whole body is calm and quiet. Then you clearly visualize an upcoming event or a goal that you desire. You allow yourself to float into the goal and see it clearly in your mind.

One of the best times for mental programming is just before you go to sleep. By verbalizing and visualizing your ideal goals or activities for the coming day immediately prior to sleeping, you program your subconscious mind to go to work on those goals all night long. Often when you wake up in the morning, you'll have insights and ideas that you can use to make those goals a reality. It's an amazing technique, and it is extremely effective. It is taught all over the world. Top athletes use this method continually to prepare for peak performance.

You can use this technique to preprogram your mind for a variety of other things as well. Say you have a problem that you're worried about. Just before you go to sleep, turn this problem over to your subconscious mind and ask for a solution. Then forget it and go to sleep. Very often when you wake up in the morning, the solution will occur to you, and it'll be crystal clear and perfect in every respect.

I use this form of mental programming to ensure that I wake up positive and energetic. This method is very simple. Just before going to sleep, I say, "When I wake up in the morning, I feel terrific." I repeat this several times. I see myself getting up the next morning feeling wonderful about myself. Every single time, I wake up in the morning feeling positive and refreshed regardless of how little sleep I might have had the night before. By using this technique, you can also wake up without an alarm clock. You can travel and wake up without jet lag no matter how much you travel. It's amazing, but these things happen to you on a regular basis when you begin to tap into the higher powers of your mind.

Emotionalizing

The fourth part of the process is emotionalizing. This is the core of the technique and the heart of the matter. This is the part that makes everything else work for you.

You are completely emotional. Everything you do is governed and controlled by your emotions in some way. Most people are slaves to their emotions. They have very little control over them. They continually react to whatever's going on around them, but this is not for you. By using your emotions deliberately and purposefully, especially by keeping them positive and focused on what you want, you can put enormous power behind your visualizations, verbalizations, and idealizations.

The more emotion you put behind a statement that you make or an image that you hold in your mind, the more rapidly that statement or picture transforms into your reality, and the greater effect it has on your thinking and behavior. The key is to get the feeling that you would experience and enjoy if your goal were already realized.

Imagine that your goal is to earn a certain amount of money. You project forward and you see yourself earning this kind of money. You see the larger house, the better car, the better clothes, the better restaurants, and the better lifestyle that you'll enjoy when you're earning this amount of money. You imagine how you would feel if you were enjoying all these ingredients of success. You create the feelings of pride, happiness, and satisfaction that you will have once you achieve this goal. Like a person soaking in a hot bath, you soak your mind in these feelings exactly as if you are already at your destination.

When you combine a mental picture plus a verbalization with an emotion, you activate your subconscious mind and through it your superconscious mind.

People who practice this technique regularly are astonished at what they accomplish, and you will be as well. Your superconscious mind, which is available to you twenty-four hours per day, will give you insights and ideas that you can use to solve your problems and achieve your goals. It will show you how to get around any obstacle. It'll bring you the information that you need at exactly the right time for you. It'll bring you flashes of insight, intuition, and hunches that enable you to make the right decisions. Your subconscious mind will also give you energy, enthusiasm, and motivation that will drive you towards your goals. The key to activating this process is to idealize, verbalize, visualize, and especially emotionalize.

Realize

The fifth step in this process is to realize—to achieve your goal, to have your wishes come true.

This is a terribly important step, and it's based on the fact that every goal takes a certain amount of time to materialize. Some goals can be achieved quickly, some are medium-term, and some are long-term. In any event, your attitude toward goal attainment has an inordinate impact on whether and when you accomplish it.

> Successful people have an attitude of calm, confident expectation. They're never rushed or hurried.

In the realization phase, after you've gone through the first four steps, you simply relax, let go of the process, and let it take care of itself in its own time. Exactly what you want and need will come to you at exactly the time that you're ready for it. This explains why successful people seem to have an attitude of calm, confident expectation. They're never rushed or hurried. They're relaxed and optimistic, and they believe that everything is conspiring to bring them exactly what they want at exactly the right time for them. This must be your attitude as well.

Accelerating the Process

You can accelerate this five-step process by using reinforcement techniques in response to the events of the day. First of all, no matter what happens, look for the good in every situation. Look for the valuable lesson. Look for what you can gain from any temporary setback or obstacle. Napoleon Hill, in his twenty-five-year study of successful men and women, found that one characteristic they all had in common was that they continually looked into every difficulty for the seed of an equal or greater benefit or advantage. They constantly looked for the silver lining to even the darkest cloud. If you are looking for something good to come from every situation, you'll tend to be positive, creative, and constructive. You'll be future-oriented. You'll be optimistic and happy. If you're convinced that you're going to benefit from everything that happens to you, not only will you maintain the attitude of the possibility thinker, but you'll almost always find something good that you can turn to your advantage.

Something else that you can do to become and remain a possibility thinker is to get up and read something uplifting and inspirational for thirty or sixty minutes each morning. The first hour of the morning is often called the rudder of the day. When you get up in the morning and instead of reading the newspaper or watching television, you read something positive, constructive, and inspiring, you set your mental stage for the rest of the day. Throughout the day, things will go better for you. You'll be calmer, more creative, and more alert. You'll be more resilient and will respond more effectively when you face the inevitable ups and downs of your daily life. Just as vigorous physical exercise in the morning will prepare you to be more resilient physically, positive mental exercise in the form of inspirational reading will prepare you to be more mentally resilient during the day.

Increase your levels of optimism by planning every day in advance.

You can increase your levels of optimism each day by planning every day in advance. The ideal time to plan is the night before. Make a list of everything you have to do in the coming day, and then go over the list and set priorities on each item. It's amazing how much better you will sleep and how much more positively you will awake when you have already preplanned your day knowing what you're going to do and in what order.

Start your day by eating healthy, nutritious foods. Eat more fruits, vegetables, and whole-grain products. Drink more fruit juices and water. Eat whole-grain breakfast cereals, muffins, and breads. Avoid fatty foods, which weigh you down and tire you out. By starting every day with a light, healthy, nutritious breakfast, you'll have more energy. You'll be more alert and positive. You'll be more eager to get on with the day. You'll be more creative because more of your blood is available to your brain. You'll see more possibilities in everything around you, and you'll become a more cheerful person.

Finally, to be a possibility thinker, get plenty of rest. Vince Lombardi, the great Green Bay Packers football coach, once wrote, "Fatigue makes cowards of us all."

Not getting enough rest predisposes you toward negativity, pessimism, and a lack of self-confidence. When you're fully rested and you're eating well, when you're continually feeding your mind with positive messages, when you're reading inspirationally and constantly visualizing your goals as a reality, you become a positive, optimistic, cheerful, and unstoppable human being. You wake up in the morning with the feeling that there is nothing that you cannot do if you put your mind to it. If you hold that thought long enough and hard enough, it becomes true.

Key Points in This Chapter

1. With possibility thinking, you look at your world in terms of possibilities rather than difficulties or problems.
2. Stress is inevitable. The only thing you can control is how you respond to it.
3. Use the five-step power process: (1) idealize, (2) verbalize, (3) visualize, (4) emotionalize, and (5) realize.
4. Always begin with a mission statement of exactly how you want to be in the future.
5. Creatively abandon things that are not consistent with your highest good.
6. Use affirmations to program your subconscious mind.
7. You control your emotions by how you choose to explain a situation to yourself.
8. Your superconscious mind will give you insights and ideas for solving problems and achieving goals.

eight

Bouncing Back from Defeat

Every successful person has experienced numerous setbacks, obstacles, and defeats, but their ability to respond positively and constructively and bounce back from these defeats ultimately determined their success. Bouncing rather than breaking will determine your success as well.

The late Abraham Zaleznik of the Harvard Business School once did a study on the role that disappointment played in life. In the past, many people had researched motivation and its relationship to success, but Zaleznik was the first person who looked at the other side of the coin. He discovered that successful people respond to disappointment differently from unsuccessful people. He concluded that the way you respond to disappointment is an extremely good indicator of your likelihood of success.

> The way you respond to disappointment is an excellent indicator of your likelihood of success.

If you're a normal, intelligent person, you'll organize every part of your life to avoid failure and disappointment. You will pre-plan as much as possible and take the necessary precautions. You will weigh and balance different situations and go in the direction that you feel offers the greatest opportunities for success. Therefore disappointment comes unbidden. Disappointment comes in spite of all your best efforts to avoid it. It becomes an inevitable and unavoidable fact of life.

As sure as the sun rises in the east and sets in the west, you are going to experience disappointments continually. The only thing that matters is what you do with the disappointment when it comes. My friend Charlie Jones says, "It's not how far you fall, but how high you bounce that counts."

Successful people respond to disappointment by taking it in stride. Unsuccessful people allow disappointments to overwhelm them. Successful people recover and continue forward. Unsuccessful people often quit and go back.

One of the most powerful principles of bouncing back from defeat lies in mental preparation. At the moment that something happens to you, you are likely to have little control over your emotions and reactions. You will react instinctively and habitually, based on your previous mental programming. It's too late to begin to think of fine and noble thoughts when you are overwhelmed with a defeat or setback.

Epictetus, the Greek Stoic philosopher, once wrote, "Circumstances do not make the man. They only reveal him to himself"—and to others for that matter. The adverse situation does not so much build your character as it reveals your character as it exists at that moment.

Mental preparation enables you to internally anticipate the inevitable disappointments that come, even though you do not know what they are or when they will arrive.

This is one of the most powerful mental techniques that you can use to keep yourself positive and moving forward. In mental preparation, you begin with the premise that when you set off toward a goal, you are going to face all kinds of problems and difficulties. In fact, if you set a high, challenging goal that takes you out of your comfort zone and sets higher standards than you have ever before achieved, you're going to meet with countless obstacles and frustrations that you cannot now imagine. It seems to go with the territory. Every time you try to be or do something different, roadblocks will appear to discourage you, scare you back into your comfort zone, and keep you at a lower level of performance.

To anticipate these inevitable difficulties, you say to yourself, "Today I will face all kinds of ups and downs, defeats and setbacks, but I will not let them get me down. Once I start toward my goal, I will be unstoppable."

Crisis Anticipation

In business consulting, I teach a way of thinking called *crisis anticipation*: decision-makers are encouraged to look down the road six to twelve months and ask, "What are some of the negative things that could happen that would derail our plans?" They then make a list of all the different things that could happen. A competitor could come out with a new product or service that was better and or cheaper. Interest rates could go up, or governments could place new taxes and regulations on their activities. Cost of fuel or raw materials could increase. A key person or persons within the organization could depart for some reason. A key customer or customers could leave and go to a competitor. Competitors could cut their prices below costs in order to take the business away. In each of these cases, the ability of the company to respond quickly and constructively could determine its viability.

The giant oil company Shell has one of the most complete forward strategic planning processes of any company in the world. They have developed over 600 scenarios that might happen in areas where they have operations around the world. As a result, they're seldom surprised by anything. They always have a backup plan ready to go. This approach to doing business in world markets has made Shell one of the most profitable and successful companies in the world.

What is successful for large corporations can be successful for you as well. Engage in regular exercises of crisis anticipation. Look down the road and think about the negative things that might happen and how you would respond to them. You'll be amazed at how much stronger and more positive you are when you've already thought through your alternative courses of action after major disappointments or setbacks.

For example, what would you do if you lost your job today? The fear of losing one's job is everywhere: statistics about the number of Americans who feared job loss in 2024 ranged from estimates of 25 to 85 percent. I once got a letter from a gentleman who told me that his fear of losing his job, which he recognized was completely irrational, was so great that it was paralyzing him and holding him back from doing the kind of work that he had to do in order to keep his job.

What is your next job going to be?

Sometimes I ask people in my audience, what is your next job going to be? For most of them, this is a real surprise. Most people have not thought about what their next job is going to be, but since the world of work is changing so dramatically and you have already changed jobs several times, it is virtually inevitable that you will change jobs again—perhaps sooner than you expect. Yet when I explain that you must be continually in preparation for your next job, it comes as a surprise to most people.

What level of knowledge, skills, and ability will you have to have at your next job in order to earn the kind of money that you want to earn in the future? If you don't think about this question in advance, you may be forced to think about it when your time has run out.

What is your next career going to be?

After people have thought about this for a few moments, I ask the second question: what is your next career going to be? What entirely new field, industry, business, or line of work are you going to be doing in five to ten years from now? The average person starting work today will have fourteen or fifteen full-time jobs, each lasting two years or more, and as many as five different careers in completely different industries requiring completely different sets of knowledge and skills. According to an educational journal published recently, as much as 99 percent of all the things you know about your current work will be obsolete and of no value in five years. Because of rapid change, your information, ideas, and even skills will be obsolete. This means that you must be continually playing down the board, as they say in chess. Another way to put it is to recall the story about Wayne Gretzky. When asked why he was perhaps the finest of all hockey players, he replied simply, "Most players are pretty good, but they go to where the puck is. I go to where the puck is going to be."

This is extremely insightful. Where is your puck going to be three to five years from now? Where is it going to be ten years from now?

FOBO

A long time perspective makes you far more effective in the short term, and those who do not think about the future cannot have one. Look down the road of your life and anticipate some of the setbacks that could occur. If you lost your job, what would you do? In working with many thousands of successful people, I have found that they all share one particular attitude: they know with complete assurance that if they lost their job, they could walk across the street and get another job tomorrow. But when most people think about losing their jobs, they go into a form of panic. They have no idea of what they would do.

Sometimes I ask my audiences what they would do if their entire industry disappeared overnight. They shake their heads and they say, that can't possibly happen, but I point out that in the 1990s, the defense industry in California collapsed in a three-year period, and over 400,000 highly competent defense engineers and executives with many years of education and experience were rendered obsolete. Their jobs were not only gone, they were gone forever. Each of these thousands of competent, capable men and women was forced into the position of going out into the marketplace, developing new skills, and going to work in an entirely new area. This is going to happen more and more often to more and more people. In 2024, the predominant fear of job loss has to do with artificial intelligence or AI. It has even acquired an acronym: FOBO—fear of being obsolete, and it affects an estimated one in five of American workers.

Similarly, if you have invested your money, you should be continually thinking about what might happen if your investments went bad and you lost it all.

As I mentioned with regard to J. Paul Getty, you must always be considering the worst possible outcome of a particular situation.

At the turn of the nineteenth century, Napoleon, the great general and later emperor of France, dominated Europe for almost twenty years. He led his armies in hundreds of battles all over the continent and only lost three in his entire career. He lost by taking his vast army to Russia in 1812 and losing it to the Russian winter. He lost the Battle of Leipzig, which led to his exile to the island of Elba, and finally in 1815, he lost the Battle of Waterloo because of a series of miscommunications with his field generals. But he won hundreds of other battles, small and large, and is considered to be one of the greatest military geniuses in history.

Napoleon had a quality that you can develop. Sometimes it is called an *extrapolatory mentality*. This was his phenomenal ability: to arrive on the field of a potential battle in advance and to think through every single possible twist and turn of the battle to its logical conclusion before it began.

Once he had done this, he could stay at his command headquarters directing the battle. No matter what news he received from any part of the battlefield, he was always ready with an instant reply. Many people thought he was a quick and brilliant thinker—which he was—but that was not the secret of his success. His secret was that he had thought through all the eventualities in advance.

Napoleon's secret: thinking through all the eventualities in advance.

This ability to think through every major situation in your life in advance is an ability that you can develop through practice. If you work with a company, think through the worst possible things that could happen six or twelve months down the road that would affect your job and your income. If you own the company, you should be doing the same. You and your spouse should be thinking on a regular basis about setbacks and disappointments that might occur and make plans to guard against them.

You read continually about people who have failed to insure properly losing their homes, cars, and sometimes all of their possessions. They fail to look into the future and ask what the consequences would be if a fire occurred in their home or if they had a traffic accident and they weren't sufficiently insured

Save Your Money

One of the smartest things that you can do to remain positive and resilient in the face of setbacks is to save at least 10 percent and even

20 percent of your income on a regular basis. Nothing gives you more strength and resilience than having a cash reserve put away in the event of an unexpected emergency, and nothing will cause you more stress and tension than living on the edge of your financial resources, unable to respond if you have a financial need or setback.

A wealthy man once wrote, "If you cannot save money, then the seeds of greatness are not in you." Your ability to save money, discipline yourself, and live within your income is a key measure of your ability to succeed in life. If you don't have the self-control to refrain from spending everything you make every single paycheck, you don't have the mental discipline to stave off difficulties when they come along. Because of the law of attraction, this negative force field of energy in your mind will also repel opportunities from you.

A man came up to me at a seminar once and told me that he had been through my two-day seminar about six years previously.

He told me about a remarkable series of events that had happened to him since. When he attended the seminar, he was a used car salesman. He had two children, and he was in his early thirties. He had far more debts than income, and he was living with his family in a rented house. After the seminar, he decided that his biggest source of worry was the fact that he was in debt and had no money in the bank, so he set a goal to get out of debt and save $30,000 over the next five years. Once he had set the goal and made a plan, he achieved his goal. In only three years, he was out of debt and he had $30,000 in the bank.

As it happened, his boss one day called him in and asked him if he was interested in a business opportunity.

The salesman was very flattered and asked his boss what he was talking about. His boss said that he had observed how much better he had become month after month in his job, and he had also heard that he had saved up some money from his income. The boss told him that he had been approached by the automobile manufacturer for a recommendation for a new car dealership in a growing part of the same city. The boss said that he was willing to back this gentleman as a full partner in this dealership if he was willing to put in his money as well. His boss helped this man set up the new dealership and assisted him with decisions about purchasing, parts, service, and staffing. After two years, his boss sold his equity back to this gentleman, so he ended up owning the dealership all by himself.

"Six years ago," he told me, "I was a used car salesman, and today I'm a millionaire." He was one of the happiest people I've ever met. He said that if he had not taken that advice from the seminar and begun saving his money and getting out of debt, he would have not been in a position to take advantage of that opportunity. He said, "Taking your seminar probably saved me twenty years of hard work and maybe even a lifetime."

To remain resilient in the face of disappointment, prepare mentally, financially, and physically in advance.

To remain strong and resilient in the face of disappointment, prepare mentally, financially, and physically in advance. Think through what might possibly happen and make plans to minimize or escape the consequences of a potential disappointment. This way of thinking is the mark of the superior individual.

Two Magic Questions

Here are two questions that you can ask to turn failure into success. I call them the two magic questions. You can apply them on a regular basis to everything you do. Ask them after every experience. The first question is, *what did I do right?* No matter what you did or how it works out, whether a success or a failure, do an instant replay of the event and assess everything you did right in that situation. No matter how badly something turns out, you did many things that were correct. If you can isolate them and identify them by thinking about them and, even better, by writing them down, you'll be preprogramming your mind to repeat the right things that you did in the next similar situation.

**Two magic questions: What did I do right?
What would I do differently**

The second magic question is, *what would I do differently?* This is an excellent question, because it forces you to think positively about what happened.

Ask yourself: if you had to do it over again, how would you change or improve your performance or behavior in that situation? What would you do more of or less of? Again, write your answers down on a piece of paper.

Each time you have a new experience, immediately sit down with a pad of paper and answer those two questions: what did I do right, and what would I do differently? The wonderful thing about these questions is that they are both positive and they both require positive responses. Underachievers almost invariably rehash their mistakes, expenses, and failures. High achievers, on the other hand, are constantly reviewing the most positive parts of their performance and planning to repeat them in subsequent events.

When you think about what you did right and what you could do differently next time, your mind will be completely positive.

Your creative juices will be flowing. You will see all kinds of opportunities and possibilities that you would have completely missed if you allowed yourself to feel sorry for yourself after an unsuccessful event.

If you're in sales, use this method after every sale. Use this method so often and so regularly that it becomes automatic. No matter how disappointed you are, you'll be automatically preprogrammed to thoroughly evaluate the situation and extract every kernel of good that you can possibly get from it.

If you're in business, you should ask these questions of yourself and your key staff on a regular basis: what did we do right, and what would we do differently next time? If you combine this method with the twenty-idea method I explained earlier, you'll be astonished at the number of powerful ideas that you come up with. They will dramatically reduce the time it takes to learn the lessons you will need for success the next time.

When you experience a disappointment, your natural reaction will be to feel a little bit stunned emotionally. You will feel as though you have been punched in your emotional solar plexus. You will feel hurt, let down, disappointed, and a bit sad. You will even have an impulse to quit that entire course of action and do something completely different. These feelings are normal and natural. The only question is, how long do they last?

When you go to for a medical exam, the doctor will ask you to engage in some aerobic exercises to get your heart rate up.

Once it is up to a particular point, the doctor will measure your resting heart rate one, two, and five minutes after the exercise. The mark of your health is how rapidly you go back to normal resting heartbeat after working out.

> Your recovery rate is everything.

Similarly, the mark of your mental health is how quickly you bounce back after experiencing disappointment. Of course it will hurt—it always hurts if what you're trying to do is important to you—but that's not the main point. The main point is how quickly you recover. Your recovery rate is everything, and if you preplan and preprogram the way I've discussed in this chapter, your recovery rate will be very fast. Remember, your recovery rate is totally determined by the way you think about what happens to you. As Shakespeare wrote, "There is nothing either good or bad but thinking makes it so."

Affirmations for Negative Situations

Here are some powerful affirmations that I've developed that you can use to take immediate mental and emotional control over a negative situation.

The first, no matter what happens, is for you to say, "I am responsible." When something goes wrong, you will naturally tend to become angry, upset, and either to blame someone or something else or to make excuses. But the instant that you say, "I am responsible," the words will neutralize your tendency to blame other people. They will neutralize your feelings of disappointment, anger, and frustration. The instant that you say, "I am responsible," your mind becomes calm and clear again, and you begin to think of positive, constructive things that you can do to minimize the damage or maximize the opportunity.

"I am responsible."

The second affirmation that I use—which has been extraordinarily helpful to me over the years, no matter what has happened and no matter how disappointed I am—is to immediately say, "Every experience is a positive experience if I view it as an opportunity for growth and self-mastery."

This statement enables you to assert full control over your emotions. Like "I am responsible," these words give you a sense of control, power, and strength: "Every situation is a positive situation if I view it as an opportunity for growth and self-mastery." Then look into the situation and ask yourself what you can possibly learn from what has happened. How can you grow? What has this situation been sent to teach you? If you had a divine force that was controlling your destiny and this force was sending you specific learning experiences to help you to be successful, what learning experience could you find contained in your current difficulty? If you're looking for a solution or a valuable lesson from every difficulty, it's not possible to be upset or angry.

Your mind can only hold one thought at a time, positive or negative. If you use the law of substitution to deliberately think about the positive aspects of the situation, you will always find them, and you will be able to turn them to your advantage.

Psychologists say that a positive mental attitude, which means a positive and constructive response to disappointments and setbacks, is largely determined by having a sense of control of your own life. You feel that you are in charge. You feel that you are in the driver's seat. You feel that you are on top of things.

Failure Is Never Final

One of the most powerful techniques to help you bounce back from failure is to put it into its proper perspective. Failure is never final, and most mistakes that you make are small relative to the great scheme of things.

If you think back, you'll probably not even be able to remember what you were worrying about a year ago, much less three or four or five years ago. The key to having a feeling of being in control is to have a clear sense of direction. This sense of direction comes from having clear specific written goals.

Another powerful technique to keep your mind positive is to simply think about your goals. When something goes wrong, think about your goals. When you lose a job or investment, think about your goals. When a sale collapses or a piece of business fails to come through, think about your goals. Your long-term goals are to be financially independent, completely healthy, to have wonderful relationships, and to do work that makes a difference in the world and do it extremely well. When you keep your mind on these goals and your specific definitions of these goals, it's almost impossible to feel upset about events that happen in the short term.

The late management consultant Peter Drucker advised people to think in terms of cycles and trends. Think in terms of ups and downs, think in terms of summers and winters, falls and springs. When you develop this long-term perspective, you're much more capable of rolling with short-term fluctuations in your fortunes. You can put things into their proper place. You can shrug and say, "What can't be cured must be endured." The great psychologist William James once wrote that the first step in dealing with any difficulty is to be willing to have it so.

Many problems in dealing with disappointments come from resistance. We engage in denial. We become angry and insist that this should not have happened, and should not have happened to *us*.

We reject it or wish that it hadn't occurred, and this resistance and denial cause most of our stress. But when you say what can't be cured must be endured, you lower your flashpoint. You become more relaxed. You become calmer, and you develop a more detached perspective. You stand back and look at the situation as though it were happening to someone else. As a result, you can become more constructive about remedying it. You don't allow yourself to get emotionally involved in every up and down of your life. Abraham Lincoln wrote that most people are just about as happy as they make up their minds to be. The spiritual text known as *A Course in Miracles* says, "I have given everything I see all the meaning it has for me." Without the meaning that you attach to an event, it has no emotional significance to you, and you can change its meaning by controlling your thinking. You can even eliminate its meaning altogether by refusing to become emotionally involved in it.

It's always up to you. Your ability to continually deal with disappointment in a positive, constructive way will do more to enable you to succeed—and will say more about you to other people—than any other single factor, and it is a learned ability.

All leaders of large organizations respond effectively to large and small crises that occur unbidden, unexpectedly, and unavoidably. You must do the same: decide in advance that no matter what happens, nothing will ever stop you. Decide in advance that although you will have countless ups and downs in the course of your life, you will keep on keeping on until you win through to your goals. When you make these decisions in advance, when you engage in mental preparation, you will be ready for the inevitable problems. You'll be fast on your feet and ready to bounce instead of break.

Key Points in This Chapter

1. The way you respond to disappointment is an excellent indicator of your likelihood of success.
2. Mental preparation enables you to anticipate disappointments.
3. Practice crisis anticipation: ask what events could happen in the future that could derail your plans.
4. It is virtually inevitable that you will have to change jobs—or careers.

5. A long time perspective makes you far more effective in the short term.
6. One of the smartest things you can do is to save 10 or 20 percent of your income on a regular basis.
7. Two magic questions: What did I do right? What would I do differently?
8. Always remember: "I am responsible."

nine

Creative Networking

The people you know—and who know you in a favorable way—will do more to determine your success, happiness, and level of achievement than any other single factor.

Relationships are everything. My friend Charlie Jones says that in five years, you will be the same as you are today except for the books you read and the people you meet. David McClelland's twenty-five years of research at Harvard University concluded that your choice of a reference group will have more to do with your success than any other single factor. McClelland looked at graduates of the university and graduates of his intensive seminars on achievement in American life. He followed these people for many years. Many of them took the information and ideas and did wonderful things with them. They built successful businesses and successful careers. But many graduates failed to turn the information and ideas into later success.

Why?

When McClelland went back and surveyed his less successful former students, he found that invariably they had returned to the same old group of people they had been associating with previously. As a result, they went back to the same old ways, the same old habits, the same old customs and manners of living, and nothing changed for them.

Your Reference Group

Your reference group is defined as the people you consider yourself to be similar to. If you belong to a church, the members of that church are part of your reference group. You consider yourself to be like them. If you belong to a particular profession, political party, or bowling league, people in those groups are parts of your reference group. You identify strongly with them. Over time, you'll adopt their attitudes, mannerisms, ways of speaking, levels of aspiration, and even their methods of dress.

> Your reference group is the people you consider yourself to be similar to.

Your reference group will exert an inordinate influence on the kind of person you become. You will adjust your goals, behaviors, and thoughts to be consistent with the way you feel they will approve of. We see this with teenagers all the time.

I've worked with countless men and women who have taken this advice to heart. They have changed their reference groups. They have begun associating with different people in different organizations. As a result, they come to think differently about themselves, and their outer worlds begin to change as well.

The law of correspondence says that your outer world will reflect your inner world. The Bible says, "As he thinketh in his heart, so is he" (Proverbs 23:7). As you see yourself and think about yourself in your subconscious mind, your outer world changes and conforms to a pattern consistent with it.

The most important impacts on your thinking and feeling will be caused by the people in your life. Successful people make lifelong habits of associating with other positive, success-oriented people. Unsuccessful people by default end up associating with other people who are not going anywhere. Both sets of people become more and more like those with whom they most identify.

> Set a goal of associating with men and women you admire, respect, and look up to.

Set a goal to begin associating in every part of your life with men and women you admire, respect, and look up to. You will associate with people who you enjoy and can learn from. You will work and socialize with people that you want your children to be like when they grow up.

When you set these standards for your interpersonal relationships, your whole life begins to improve almost immediately.

The Law of Indirect Effort

Several principles apply to building and maintaining relationships. Perhaps the most important is the *law of indirect effort*. This law says that you achieve more with people indirectly than directly. Let me give you some examples.

> The law of indirect effort: you achieve more with people indirectly than directly.

You know that if you want to have a friend, you must first be a friend. If you want to impress other people, instead of trying to impress them, which is the direct way, you should instead be impressed by them, which is the indirect way of building relationships. The indirect way of getting people to like you is to like them first. The way to get people to admire and respect you is to admire and respect them in advance.

The law of compensation seems to apply directly to relationships.

The more you put in, the more you get out, the more and better things you do for other people, the more and better things other people will do for you.

We have entered into the era of the go-giver rather than the go-getter. Nowhere is this more important than in relationships. Many people think that a key to success is to get around other successful people and exploit this relationship. Over time I've learned that it's much better to become a successful person that other people want to be around. When you go to work on yourself and become a better person, other better people will want to associate with you. This is the indirect way. Some people say they want to marry a rich person. If you want to marry a rich person, work on yourself to become the kind of person that a rich person would want to marry.

In every case, the law of indirect effort applies. Everything begins with yourself. There have been many studies of social climbers: people who have joined clubs and organizations in an attempt to get around successful people. Invariably they fail. Why? Because like attracts like. People are naturally attracted to people who are at the same level. If you have not worked on yourself to bring yourself up to a particular level, you cannot take a shortcut and just begin associating with people at that level. They will not be interested in you, and you'll only end up looking and feeling foolish.

Your network is composed of the people over whom you can exert some influence and who can exert influence over you.

Your network is composed of the people you know, both directly and indirectly, over whom you can exert some influence and who can exert some influence over you. The most successful people are those who know the greatest number of other successful people. They get to know a lot of other successful people by deliberate design, not by accident, and so can you.

I've worked with men and women who have moved from one city to another or one industry to another. In a short time, they've become some of the best known and most respected people in that industry. Why? Because they use the principles of creative networking that I'll be talking about in this chapter. They immediately went to work to form new, positive reference groups. They placed an extraordinarily high emphasis on relationships, and they developed as many high-quality relationships as possible within the shortest period of time. In my own experience moving from one city to another, I've found that by getting involved with certain clubs and organizations, I was able to make more progress in a couple of years than many people had made in ten or twenty years.

Even before you begin to join groups and organizations, the core of your personal contacts should be your Master Mind network. This is a small group of four or five people with whom you meet and interact on a regular basis. Napoleon Hill, author of *Think and Grow Rich*, concluded after decades of studying success that the formation of what he called a "Master Mind" was the critical step that enabled countless men and women to turn the corner from wealth and obscurity to fame and power.

You form a Master Mind by meeting on a regular basis, preferably weekly or even more often, with other people who think as you do. You must be very selfish about these relationships. Your most valuable asset is your time, and people are enormously time-consuming. You cannot have an unlimited number of high-quality relationships: there are simply not enough hours in the day or enough days in the month. You must be very selective about the people with whom you associate, and you must choose them carefully. The Baron de Rothschild said, "Make no useless acquaintances." This may sound cold, but your life is precious, and it is made up of the minutes and hours of each day. You cannot afford to throw them away on useless relationships with people you cannot help and who cannot help you.

You must be extremely careful in this respect.

Highly successful people are often described as loners. This does not mean that they're isolated, antisocial individuals. They are loners in that they're highly selective about whom they spend time with. They don't drink coffee with whoever is sitting there or go out for lunch with whoever happens to be walking out the door at the same time. They carefully build and maintain high-quality relationships, and they fastidiously avoid negative people who might hold them back.

If forming a Master Mind relationship is a key to success, the flip side is getting away from negative or toxic people. Negative people are the primary source of most of life's problems. They are a major source of stress and unhappiness. They do more to diminish joy in life than any other single factor.

> Negative people are the primary source of most of life's problems.

It's much easier to bounce back from financial loss or career changes than it is to deal with perennially negative people. A single negative relationship can be harmful enough to cut off your chances of achieving your full potential. Choose your relationships with care.

The Master Mind

You form a Master Mind network by approaching one or two people that you admire and who are going in the same direction you are. They may be in your field or outside your field. They may be younger or older than you, of the same sex or of a different sex. It doesn't really matter, as long as you have good chemistry. All that matters is that they have positive mental attitudes and are generally constructive and future-oriented. They have goals of their own that they're working on each day. They are open, curious, and eager. They read books, listen to self-development audio programs, and associate with other like-minded people.

When you get together with these associates on a regular basis, you will have ideas and insights to share about what is going on in the world. You may not even talk about your particular business, but t spending time around other positive people causes you to function more creatively, gives you more energy, makes you more positive, and engenders higher levels of enthusiasm in you.

The critical factor in your Master Mind network is that you laugh a lot with the other people. It is the key measure of your success in relationships. People who laugh a lot together are usually very helpful to one another, and the people you like and enjoy most will always be those with whom you find yourself joking and laughing.

The most important Master Mind network that you ever enter into is with your spouse: a husband and wife together or a couple can be the most powerful Master Mind of all. If they are completely attuned to each other and supportive of each other's goals and aspirations, they can be a tremendous help to each other and to themselves as a couple. People who are in excellent relationships with someone they describe as their best friend are some of the happiest, most successful, and most blessed people in our society.

By the way, you can have more than one Master Mind network. Some people will have a Master Mind network with regard to their families, another with regard to their hobbies or sports. Some will have a Master Mind network that is specifically focused on their work or career. You can have separate or interlocking Master Mind groups with separate people or with people who are involved with you in more than one area.

In any case, the more you interact with other positive people, the more positive and productive you'll be. Constantly talking with and sharing your experiences with others gives you ideas and insights from their previous experiences and helps you to keep a healthy perspective on what you're doing.

The major focus of networking developed by most high-achieving men and women and self-made millionaires is regular involvement with groups, clubs, and associations with members who can be of some assistance to them in their particular field.

The 100 List

Here's a great exercise for you. Over the course of the next six to twelve months, make a list in a spiral notebook of the 100 most important people in your community. As you gather these names from the newspapers, conversations, news broadcasts, and your work, begin to think of how you could get to meet and know these people.

> Eighty-five percent of the best jobs in America are filled through contacts.

As I said earlier, the more people you know and who know you and think about you in a positive way, the more successful you will be. Eighty-five percent of the best jobs in America are filled through contacts, not through want ads or recruitment agencies. Someone has the need for a particular job and they let it be known within their network. The word goes out from person to person, and an individual who could never be found any other way often surfaces and, as the result of personal connections, is directed to a job for which they're well suited. Many people have found that by broadening their contacts as much as possible, when they did change careers, they happened to know the right person who was in the right place to make the right introduction to get the right job that saved the individual years of hard work in moving to that same level of responsibility and income.

Once you have your list of 100 people, add to it regularly, and network systematically with these people. Once you have a name, think of how you could communicate with that person. The simplest way is to write a letter expressing your opinion on something that they're involved in or expressing your congratulations on their success for a recent achievement. Don't expect the person to call you back or to come to your door to meet with you. You are in the business of sowing seeds. Sometime down the road, you may see that that person has done something else, and you can write them another letter. Over time, these little efforts will begin to bear fruit.

I write letters continually to people I meet throughout the country.

I always send a copy of a poem, sometimes a book, sometimes an audio program—something that I feel the other person would enjoy. I've done this over the years for hundreds and perhaps thousands of people, and now, wherever I go, people come up to me and remind me that I wrote to them and I sent them something, often years ago.

Once I was in Washington at a high-level conference. A senior person from one of the largest organizations in the nation's capital came up to me and reminded me that I had written to him and sent him something five years before. He still remembered. Over time, I got to know him very well. He has now introduced me to a variety of other powerful and well-known people. These new relationships have turned out to be very enjoyable and productive for me, and they all started with me sitting down and writing a letter to a single person.

Join a Club

Decide right now to join one or two clubs or associations. Of course, the first one that you should join should be the one for your profession or occupation. If you are in real estate, join the real estate board. If you are an entrepreneur, join an entrepreneurial association. If you're in sales, join a club like Sales & Marketing Executives International.

When you join a professional association, don't make the mistake of merely attending the meetings and going home. This is what 80 to 90 percent of the people do. They may get some benefit out of their association, but nowhere nearly as much as you can receive if you get involved. Believe me, I know. When you join a club or organization, get the membership book, and look at the various committees. Ask around and find out which of the committees is most active and most important to the organization.

Sometimes it's the membership committee. Sometimes it's the government relations committee. Sometimes it's the education committee or the fundraising committee. Whatever it is, find out what committee seems to have the greatest impact on the health and growth of the organization and then volunteer to serve on that committee. When you get onto that committee, develop the habit of raising your hand; volunteer for assignments, volunteer to write things, volunteer to do work that needs to be done. The rule is this: in every organization, less than 10 percent of the people will do all the work. On any committee, less than 20 percent of the people will do more than 80 percent of the work on that committee. But the best committees have the best and most important people in the association. You want these people as part of your reference group. You want to form relationships with these people. You want their contact information, and you want them to be part of your professional network.

One great advantage of serving on a committee for your association is that you get an opportunity to perform in front of your peers without ever attempting to impress them or to get them to give you anything or do anything for you. Every time you accept a responsibility and fulfill it completely, they make note of it. They may not say anything aside from an occasional thanks or congratulations, but they're making mental notes which will serve you in good stead later on.

If you have any fears about public speaking, plan right now to get over them. Your ability to make a presentation to a small group, stand up and give a talk, or chair a meeting can do more to bring you to the attention of people who can help you than almost anything else.

I have urged people over the years to take a Dale Carnegie course or join Toastmasters International. By doing so, you'll be thoroughly trained in how to speak on your feet. They will teach you how to design a talk with a beginning, a middle, and an end. They'll show you how to speak in a variety of different situations. By the law of attraction, the better you get at speaking, the more you will attract people and opportunities to enable you to speak to larger and larger groups.

The Power of the Chamber

Some years ago, I moved from one city to another. I was invited by a friend to get involved on the education committee of the Chamber of Commerce. Since I was interested in education and I was somewhat alone in the city, I volunteered my time. I began working on reports on education and how the liaison between business and schools could be improved.

Since I had a lot of time on my hands in the evenings, I worked hard on these reports and I did a good deal of research. The reports were well received, so much so that the others eventually turned over the research and report writing to me completely.

Within six months, there was a statewide conference of Chambers of Commerce. Education became a major theme. They needed someone to act as a master of ceremonies for the combined work of more than 100 chambers for an entire day. As it happened, they asked me if I would volunteer my services. By the end of the day, I had been brought to the attention of some of the most important businesspeople in the entire state. I was asked if I would volunteer to perform other functions. Eventually, I was invited onto the elite committee of the overall Chamber of Commerce, the business government relations committee. Soon I was working with businesspeople at the highest levels of government.

These activities came to the attention of some of the most powerful businesspeople in the state. One of them contacted me and offered me a high-level job. In this job, I was able to leapfrog over people who had worked ten or fifteen years to get to the same position.

Two and a half years later, I was hired away at double the salary by another major businessman, who had seen me performing at one of the committee meetings. I look back, and I'm amazed that I was able to go from knowing no one to mixing with the best known and most powerful people in the entire state, and it all took less than two years.

Eventually, I was invited to head up election campaigns and fundraising drives. I was invited to work as a senior member with the United Way.

I was written up in the newspapers, and doors of opportunity were opened up to me in both business and government. It all started with volunteering my time and my energies to make a contribution to an organization that I believed in.

Here's something very important that I learned: the great majority of people, being selfish, are always thinking of how they can personally and immediately gain from any interaction, but this is not for you. Your job is to look for ways to put in. Your job is to look for ways to contribute.

I have worked with some extremely wealthy men and women over the years. I will never forget a billionaire turning to me at the end of a meeting and privately asking, "Is there anything that I can do for you?" Later, another man worth more than $500 million asked me the same thing: "Is there any way that I can help you?"

When I went to work for a man worth more than $800 million, in our second or third meeting, he too asked me if there was anything that he could do to help me.

Over the years, I've seen that the most powerful men and women at every level of society got there by continually looking for ways to help other people to achieve their goals. This is an extension of the law of sowing and reaping. As I've already observed, the law of sowing and reaping is formulated in a particular order: it is *not* the law of reaping and sowing. The law of sowing and reaping says that first you put something in, and then you get something out. It is not the other way around.

The Law of Indirect Compensation

Here's one of the great discoveries of the centuries: the more you give of yourself without expectation of return, the more return will come to you from the most unexpected sources.

> The more you give of yourself without expectation of return, the more return will come to you from unexpected sources.

Most people think that if they do something good for a person or group, their rewards should come back directly from that person or group, but that's not the way the universe works. When you do something good for someone else, you never have to worry. As long as you control the sowing, the universe will take care of the reaping. Your good will often come to you from a completely unexpected source and at a completely unexpected time. All you have to do is be sure that you are continually putting in. The getting out will take care of itself.

As a professional speaker, I work with groups and associations all over the country. Without fail, the best people in every association are the ones who attend virtually every meeting. They always take the time and make the sacrifice. They always sit on the committees and volunteer to help in any way possible.

I learned another thing.

Many times a member of an association will be elected the national president. As the president, they will have to spend maybe half of their time traveling around the country voluntarily without pay on association business. You would think that this would really cut into the person's ability to make a living, but it seems to be exactly the opposite. Every association president that I've spoken to found that they made more money, did better in their careers, and made more progress in their field in the year that they took off to work for the association than in any other year of their work lives. Again, the more you put in without expectation of reward, the more you get back from the most unexpected sources.

Relationship Maintenance

We often work hard to form a relationship, but if you're not careful, you'll start to take it for granted. Relationships naturally tend toward entropy, meaning that you will let the energy run down. You'll stop doing the things that you had done earlier to build the relationship. You may drop off in communicating with that person. You will just assume that everything is going along fine; since you are so busy, you don't need to do anything to maintain the relationship. But all relationships are a function of the time invested in them: you can only increase its value by investing more time in it. This applies to relationships with your spouse, children, staff members, and especially with your friends and associates on a personal and professional level. There's no alternative to personal time invested in building and maintaining a relationship. You must be sensitive to the factor of entropy and constantly work to counter it.

Many businesspeople work hard to develop high-quality customer relationships. Then they begin to take them for granted and go off to work on new relationships. Six months later, they're astonished to find that their first customer has gone to a competitor. Your customer relationships are some of your most important assets. Once you've made all the efforts involved in developing a customer relationship, it's essential to develop a plan for relationship maintenance. Make sure that you are regularly doing things that keep that relationship alive and growing.

Mentoring

The final form of creative networking has to do with mentoring. Your success is often determined by a person whom you know and who knows you and helps you on a regular basis.

This can happen either by accident by design. Believe me, design is better. At each stage of your life, you can benefit from the advice and experience of someone who is further along than you. My life has been dramatically affected by the men who have been there to give me guidance and advice as I have grown up and gone into business at various levels. This type of relationship can have a major impact on your success as well.

Many people are fuzzy about mentoring relationships. Let me explain what they are. A mentor is like an uncle: an older friend who is wiser and more experienced than you and who will give you the guidance and advice from time to time that can help you to avoid pitfalls that might hold you back.

> A mentor is a wiser and more experienced
> friend who will give you guidance and advice.

As it happens, most mentors, most successful people from whom you would like to get advice, are very busy. When you decide that you would like a particular person to mentor you, you should contact that person with a specific question or need. Successful men and women are always willing to help other people who want to be successful, but they don't have a lot of time, so you should only ask for five or ten minutes.

The best way to approach a prospective mentor for the first time is with a short list of key questions about current decisions in your life and career. Ask for specific advice about a specific situation. Don't approach a mentor by asking personal questions about their own life and experiences. People are not interested in exposing their innermost feelings to someone they've never met. So when you ask a few specific questions, you're testing the waters.

You are looking for a certain form of chemistry. You are looking for a person that you like, respect, and feel comfortable with and who likes you and will be willing to help you in the future. For this reason, you must go slowly at first. Only ask for a few minutes, then get on with your business and let the potential mentor get on with theirs.

Here's the key to developing the mentor mentee relationship: when you get advice, follow it. Don't ask for specific advice, do nothing about it, and then attempt to come back for even more advice. This just convinces the prospective mentor that you are wasting their time. Instead, if the person suggests that you take a particular action, try it. If the mentor suggests that you read a book, read it.

If they suggest that you listen to an audio program, get it and listen to it. If they suggest that you take a particular course, take the course.

As a professional speaker, I have many people approaching me to be a mentor to them. I respectfully decline these invitations because of the approach they take. They often call up wanting me to take complete charge of their lives and spend many hours of time guiding, counseling, directing them, and helping them in their careers. But a prospective mentor has an extremely busy life of his own and cannot consider the possibility of spending large blocks of time with a complete stranger.

The good news is that if you go slowly and follow the advice given to you by a mentor, they will begin to realize that investing time in you is worthwhile.

They will be willing to spend more time with you to help you even further. Eventually, a very good relationship can develop.

You may have more than one mentor at the same time, and you may have sequential mentors. As one mentor serves their purpose and you evolve and grow in your career, it's often time to move on to another one who is even further along than the first.

In any case, relationships are everything. Your job is to become a relationship creating individual. Look for every way possible—in your personal reference groups, in your Master Mind networks, in clubs and associations, and with mentors—to form and maintain high-quality relationships. Most successful men and women owe their success to the fact that at an earlier time, they established and maintained a high-quality relationship that eventually opened a key door for them.

This can happen to you when you use creative networking and you have contact information for hundreds of valuable names that you can call upon because you've already built a bridge with these people. It gives you a tremendous feeling of personal power and self-confidence.

Key Points in This Chapter

1. Your reference group will exert an inordinate influence on the kind of person you become.
2. The law of indirect effort: you achieve more with people indirectly than directly.
3. Your network is composed of the people you know, both directly and indirectly, over whom you can exert some influence and who exert influence over you.
4. A Master Mind network is a small group of people with whom you meet and can share inspiration.
5. The most important Master Mind network you will ever enter into is with your spouse.
6. Eighty-five percent of the best jobs in America are filled through contacts.
7. The more you give of yourself without expectation of return, the more return will come to you from unexpected sources.
8. Success is often determined by a mentor: a wiser and more experienced individual who knows you and helps you on a regular basis.

ten

Character Makes the Difference

The law of correspondence is perhaps the most important of all laws in determining your success in life. As I've already explained, this law says that your outer world reflects your inner world: whatever you are on the inside, you will eventually see the results of it on the outside.

This law applies to every part of your external existence. Your inner world of knowledge and preparation will determine your outer world of wealth and career success. Your inner world of personality development will determine your outer world of friendships and relationships. Your inner attitudes toward health and fitness will determine the condition of your physical body. Your inner beliefs and expectations will determine your attitudes and your behaviors toward other people. Your outer world will always reflect your inner world.

> The ultimate aim of all human action is happiness.

Virtue and Happiness

Aristotle, perhaps the greatest of all philosophers, wrote almost 2,400 years ago that the ultimate aim of all human action was happiness.

He concluded that everything that a person did was to achieve happiness of some kind. Sometimes people were successful, sometimes they were unsuccessful, but happiness was always the target. He concluded that every act in between was merely a step in the direction of happiness. A person wants to get a good job. Why? So he can earn good money. Why? So he can get a nice home and a nice car. Why? So he can have a good relationship and a nice family. Why? So that he can have a rich home life. Why? So that he can ultimately be happy. Everything is aimed at happiness.

Aristotle's major contribution in this area was his discovery that only the good can be happy, and only the virtuous can be good. This is one of the most important observations in history. Similarly, in my many years of research into philosophy and psychology, I have found that only people who are genuinely good inside can be happy for any period of time. In my years of work in the foundation qualities of self-confidence, I found that only men and women with solid internal values which they refuse to compromise had the kind of unshakable self-confidence that enabled them to take on the world.

> The most important single quality for success is integrity.

In fact, the fastest way to regain your self-confidence is to get back in touch with your innermost values and convictions and refuse to compromise them. The truth is that the solution to virtually all human problems is a return to values. In almost every case, our problems are caused by our straying away from what we know to be good and right and true. The most important single quality for success in any area of life is integrity.

Aristotle concluded that a life based on honesty, integrity, courage, generosity, and persistence would lead to a good life. I used to think that integrity was the key value in itself. Then a wise and wealthy man pointed out to me that it was merely the value that guaranteed all the others. That was a real breakthrough.

Integrity is the foundation value upon which all of your other values are built. If you have integrity, it means that you'll remain consistent with your other values. If you don't have integrity, you will compromise them at the slightest temptation.

In our strategic planning sessions, both for corporations and for individuals, we start off by asking people to define and clarify their values. What are your values? What do you believe in? What do you stand for? What will you not stand for?

> Clearly defining your values is the starting point of building and maintaining character.

Clearly defining your values is the starting point of building and maintaining the kind of character that makes people want to associate with you and leads you inevitably to a good life. When you have a high level of character based on firm values, you'll become a genuinely good person; as a result, you'll be happy inside no matter what is going on around you.

Prioritizing Your Values

How do you tell what your values are? It's simple. Your values are always and only expressed in your actions and behavior, especially when you're under pressure. You can only do one thing at a time, and you always have to choose. You always choose what is most valuable to you at that particular moment. It's been said that you are a choosing organism. The thing that distinguishes you from all other creatures is that you make choices. Every part of your life is the result of a choice, either good or poor. And every choice you make is based on what you consider to be the most valuable and important consideration at that time.

> Your values are always and only expressed in your actions and behavior.

You don't really need more than about three to five key values. These are the ones that you consider to be more important than anything else. But once you've defined them, you need to organize them in order of priority, because the order in which you prioritize your values is terribly important as well. It determines the kind of person you are and the kind of life you live. Let me give you an example.

First, a higher-order value always takes precedence over a lower-order value. Every action you take, every decision you make is based on your dominant values at the time.

Let me give you an example. Imagine that we have done a values clarification exercise for two people, person A and person B. Person A comes up with his three values in order: (1) family, (2) health, and (3) career. This person is saying that he puts his family ahead of his health and career. If he has to choose between family and career, family comes first. If he has to choose between health and career, health comes first.

Person B has the same three values, only in a slightly different order. Person B has career as his first value. The second value is family, and his third value is health. This means that person B will put his career ahead of his family if he has to choose. He'll put his career and his family ahead of his health if he has to choose.

Will there be a difference between person A and person B? Will there be a small difference or a large difference? Would you like to be friends with person A, or would you like to be friends with person B? Finally, would you be able to tell person A from person B if you met them?

Person B, who puts his career as his number one value, will be a totally different human being from person A, who puts his family as his number one value. The order of family, health, and career is a life-enriching organization of values. A person who lives consistently with them will be a far happier person than one who places his career ahead of family and especially ahead of health. Select both your values and their order of importance with care.

Select both your values and their order of importance with care.

To Thine Own Self . . .

Once you've determined your values, your level of integrity determines how rigidly you adhere to them. You do not compromise a value when it's convenient. A person is only defined by what they do, not what they say. Many people don't realize that it is not what they wish, hope, say, or intend that determines their true values. It's only what you actually do when push comes to shove, when you have to choose under pressure, that tells you who you really are inside.

It's essential to your success and happiness that you be impeccably honest with everyone you deal with, both in your personal life and in your career.

Nothing will earn you the support of people faster than to develop the reputation of being a person of character and integrity. At the same time, nothing will sabotage your career faster than developing the reputation of being the kind of person that others cannot rely on.

Honesty means that you are always true to the best that is in you. Shakespeare wrote, "To thine own self be true, and it must follow, as the night the day, thou canst not then be false to any man." Being true to yourself is the starting point of developing a high character. This means that you always tell the truth to yourself. You don't delude yourself or play games with your own mind. You don't try to believe things that are completely impossible. You don't wish and hope that things would be different than they are. You are absolutely true to yourself.

Being true to yourself also means that you always do your best at whatever job or responsibility you take on. Every job contains the signature of the person who did it. Honesty and integrity on the inside are expressed as quality and excellence in your work. You can tell what you are made of on the inside by the amount of time and attention that you put into doing the best job possible at everything you do.

Integrity means that you are always truthful, straightforward, and honest with everyone. One of the most important parts of character is living in truth with others at home and at work.

If you ask a person if he or she is honest, almost everyone will say that they are.

Most people do not lie, cheat, steal, or engage in dishonest behaviors, but being truly honest means that you are honest with everyone. This means that you never lie. You never stay in a situation that is wrong for you. You never compromise your integrity by biting your lip and refusing to say what you truly think and feel.

The honest person sets peace of mind as their highest goal. Once you have set peace of mind as your organizing principle, you plan all your other goals around it. Honesty means that you refuse to compromise your peace of mind for anything or anyone. You only do and say the things that you feel to be right and honest in every situation. You listen to yourself and trust your inner voice. You listen to your intuition and let it guide you to do and say the right things at the right time.

When you sit quietly by yourself, you have a deep inner sense of peace and oneness with the universe. This is living in truth with yourself and others.

In his essay "Self-Reliance," Ralph Waldo Emerson wrote, "Guard your integrity as a sacred thing." He went on to say, "Nothing is at last sacred, but the integrity of your own mind." Truthfulness is the indispensable condition of the development of character, and the development of character must be a central aim of your entire life.

As far back as the days of Aristotle, the purpose of education was the development of the character of the young. Today in America, many young people have not been brought up with a clear sense of right and wrong. Many people have been told that values are relative.

Value relativity leads down a blind alley. It is ultimately disastrous to the person who buys into it. Values are not relative. There are values that are life enhancing, and there are values that are life debasing. If a value is good, it adds to the quality of your life and relationships. Otherwise it is not a good value, and it is to be avoided.

Living in truth means facing the truth about yourself and the world around you. You face the truth about your work and your relationships. You look yourself directly in the eye, and you live consistently with your innermost convictions.

You don't play games with yourself or wish and hope that things could be different than they are. Integrity means accepting that your world can only get better when you get better. Nothing and no one is going to come along and change things for you. If you want things to change, you are going to have to make the changes yourself.

Integrity means accepting that your marriage only gets better when you become a better spouse. Your business only gets better when you become a better manager or executive. Your sales and customers only get better when you become a better salesperson.

> With few exceptions, people don't change.

Honesty especially means that you don't go through life wishing, hoping, and expecting that people will change or be different from who they are. With few exceptions, people don't change.

In fact, under pressure, people become even more so. If a person has an aggravating personality, under pressure he will become even more aggravating. If a person is stubborn or dogmatic, under pressure she'll become even more so. If a person has a small tinge of dishonesty, under pressure he'll become totally dishonest.

Honesty in our fast-moving world also means seeing the world as it is, not as you wish it were. Today, with the explosion of information and technology, many people think that they can make a token effort to keep up with the growth of knowledge in their field, but this is not enough for the honest person, who realizes that you have to run just to stay in the same place.

Outstripping Change

Jack Welch of General Electric once said that if the rate of change outside your organization is greater than the rate of change inside your organization, the end is in sight. That applies to you as a person as well. As we have already seen, all over the United States people are being laid off by the thousands. In almost every case, they have allowed their levels of knowledge and skill to decline to the point where their companies could no longer afford to keep them. Many of these people were not completely honest with themselves. They did not continually upgrade their knowledge and skills so they could continue to add value to their companies.

They hoped that the dramatic changes in the national and international economies would not affect them; as a result, they got caught in the massive layoffs.

In April 2024, Aki Ito, writing for *Business Insider*, drew this picture of the white-collar job market:

> Among [the] lowest earners—those who make less than $55,000—the hiring rate has held up well. At 1.5%, it's still above pre-pandemic levels. But among those who make more than $96,000? It's pretty depressing. Hiring has slowed to a dismal 0.5%, less than half the peak it reached in mid-2022. Excluding the dip in the early months of the pandemic, that's the worst it's been since 2014. If you make a six-figure salary, it really is a bad time to be looking for a job.

This is likely to remain true for white-collar professionals who don't get busy upgrading themselves.

Honesty means that acknowledging that your income is totally determined by your ability to contribute value to your company and, through your company, to your customers. An individual must generate $3 of bottom line profit for every $1 of income they hope to earn from an organization. If you're not currently generating this return, your job is a prime candidate for outsourcing, downsizing, or eliminating. Honesty is accepting this fact and doing everything in your power to maintain and increase your value.

True honesty means never expecting to get more out than you put in. You never expect to get something for nothing. You don't gamble or buy lottery tickets, which in a way are acts of dishonesty: attempts to get something for nothing. The truly honest person never attempts to get rewards without working or to get rich quick and easy.

Honesty and character also mean avoiding the temptation toward the quick fix. In America today, millions of people are attracted to the quick fix. They feel that problems that have taken many months and years to develop in their lives can be solved with some silver bullet. They are impatient, and they want immediate results. If they are employees or executives, they want new and better jobs, and they want them immediately.

They're always looking for shortcuts, and as a result, they're always frustrated and unhappy.

Trust Is Central

As I said in the previous chapter, relationships are central to a happy, healthy, prosperous life, and all relationships are based on trust. Trust is the glue that holds relationships together. You can have all kinds of difficulties with another person, but as long as trust and respect are still there, the relationship can endure. But if anything ever happens to the trust, the relationship can fall apart quickly, like a house of cards. All business relationships are based on trust. All relationships that involve money depend upon the word of the borrower or the creditor. All relationships with your bankers, suppliers, customers, staff, and everyone else are based on that critical element of trust. Men and women of high integrity are extremely fastidious about the levels of trust that they've built and maintained.

They're extremely careful about their credit and their financial commitments and arrangements. They always keep their word. They're extremely careful about their banking relationships, credit cards, bills, and all monies that they owe at all times.

All relationships are based on trust.

At one point, because of an economic downturn, two friends of mine in different businesses were forced into bankruptcy, but the outcomes were completely different. The first friend had been meticulously careful about all of his bills and finances throughout his career. He had always paid at least the minimum amounts on his charge cards. If ever had a financial problem, he went to the person or bank affected and rearranged the repayment and interest terms. When he was finally forced into bankruptcy by a massive, unexpected financial default, over which he had no control, he had to go to court, give up all his assets and emerge penniless.

But within seven days, his major creditors had approached him and offered him credit cards, money, loans, offices, a place to live, and a new car. His bankruptcy hardly affected him at all except that it removed a great burden of debt from his financial back.

My other friend was not so lucky. While he was having financial problems, he continually fiddled around with his creditors. He refused to make payments and wrote checks for which there were insufficient funds. He avoided his creditors when they phoned, and he eventually changed his phone number. He moved and didn't tell anybody his address. He treated people who had trusted him by lending him money as if they were stupid. When he went bankrupt, no one would touch him with a ten-foot pole. It would take him years, probably ten years, of rebuilding, even to get a credit card. Until then, he had to pay cash for everything, including his rent.

In sales, trust is the foundation of all relationships. A person will not buy from you until he or she trusts you completely. Top salespeople spend a good deal of time building high-quality trust relationships with clients before even attempting to sell their products or services.

An association I belong to once commissioned a survey of customers. They asked them what they looked for in a salesperson before they decided to make a purchase. More than 80 percent of the respondents said that they looked for honesty and integrity in a salesperson above all other qualities. When asked what they meant by honesty and integrity in a salesperson, the customers replied that this meant that the salesperson put their interest first. They believed that the salesperson would keep their word. They believed the salesperson's claims about the product.

They believed that the salesperson would do what they said he would do and that the company would fulfill any commitments that the salesperson made. They had a high level of trust in the salesperson and in everything they did or said. Interestingly, the quality of the product or service was not mentioned. When customers were asked about this, they explained that most products or services at a particular level are quite similar. The key area of differentiation in selling today is the quality of the trust that the salesperson builds and maintains for the customer.

Truthfulness: The Essence of Character

The real essence of character and the obvious expression of honesty and integrity is truthfulness. If you are completely truthful with yourself and everyone else, you'll automatically be a person of high character. In our society, opportunities are attracted to men and women of character.

Doors are opened for men and women of character, and resources are made available to them. For those without character, doors are closed and opportunities are withheld.

The most important thing you can instill in your children is a sense of honesty and the habit of truthfulness in everything they do or say.

It's amazing how much better relationships are between parents and children when they trust each other, and of course, it's exactly the same between husbands and wives: truthfulness and honesty between a couple requires fidelity and straightforwardness at all times. If a couple is ideally suited, they absolutely trust each other and are each other's best friends. There is no one that they would talk to or express themselves more honestly with than the other. Character, integrity, and honesty are the foundation qualities of any excellent relationship.

Kant's Universal Maxim

There's a wonderful test that you can give yourself on a regular basis to measure the height of your character. It's based on the universal maxim of Immanuel Kant, the eighteenth-century German philosopher. He said that you should live your life as though your every act were to become a universal law.

In other words, you should do everything you do exactly as if everyone else should do exactly the same thing. This is the true test of whether or not your behavior is good. It is the true test of a value or decision. What kind of a society would it be if everyone lived consistent with what you espouse? Many of the problems in society today would not exist if this test were applied regularly in the areas of crime, education, and business.

Here are some questions you can ask yourself on a regular basis: First, what kind of a world would it be if everyone in it were just like me? Would this be a better world to live in?

If everyone in the world were just like you, would this be a happier, healthier, more prosperous, and more harmonious world or not?

Then ask yourself, what kind of a country would my country be if everyone in it were just like me? What kind of a country would this be if everybody in it behaved exactly the way you do? If everyone did the things that you do every hour of every day, would this be the finest country in the world, or are there some things that you might want to change?

The third question is, what kind of a company would my company be if everybody in it were just like me? Look around and ask yourself if your company would be more prosperous and harmonious if everybody in it did their work exactly the way that you do all day long.

The final question is, what kind of a family would my family be if everyone in it were just like me? Would your family be a wonderful place to live and grow up in? Would everybody in your family thrive and be happier and more successful? Would you have the kind of family that other people would admire and want to be like?

No one can completely answer yes to all of these questions. Each of us is a work in progress. Each of us has a long way to go. Each of us has a lot of work to put in on ourselves. Someone once said, "I'm a self-made man, but if I had to do it over, I'd bring in a little help."

You and I are all self-made, but we have a few things we could improve.

We all need to set higher standards for ourselves. We all need to work continually on the development of our characters. We need to strive to become better people. We can never allow ourselves to be complacent at any level of accomplishment. We have to keep raising the bar on ourselves.

Superior people look upon themselves as role models. They imagine that everyone is watching them even when no one is. If they work for a company, they imagine their boss sitting next to them, observing them, and filling out an annual performance appraisal every minute of every day. They set far higher standards for themselves than anyone else could.

When you set high standards for yourself and decide to live consistently with your highest values and deepest convictions, you begin to feel wonderful about yourself. You stop compromising yourself and your relationships. You speak straightforwardly and honestly to everyone. You practice absolute truthfulness with yourself and others. As a result, your courage and confidence go up. You feel terrific about yourself. You have a tremendous feeling of inner power and strength. The more consistently you live with the highest values you know, the finer the character you will develop.

Key Points in This Chapter

1. The ultimate aim of all human action is happiness.
2. Aristotle's great discovery: only the good can be happy, and only the virtuous can be good.
3. Integrity is the foundation value upon which all other values are built.
4. Clearly defining your values is the starting point of building character.

5. Being true to yourself means always doing your best at whatever job you take on.
6. Honesty means that you don't go through life wishing, hoping, and expecting that people will change or be different from who they are.
7. All relationships are built on trust.
8. Kant's universal maxim: live your life as though your every act were to become a universal law.

eleven

Developing Personal Power

There are three qualities that are essential to your success. They are possessed by the highest performing men and women throughout history right down to our present day. They are the foundation of personal power and a superior personality. Fortunately, they can all be learned.

These three qualities are *self-discipline*, *courage*, and *persistence*. These three qualities are like a triangle. Each of them reinforces the others. Each is indispensable to the others. None can exist unless the others have been developed to a certain level.

> ### The Foundations of Personal Power
> 1. Self-discipline
> 2. Courage
> 3. Persistence

Aristotle's work on happiness and human character concluded that if you find yourself without a particular virtue or value you admire, you can develop it in yourself by studying it and acting as if you had it already.

In fact, any virtue of character that you wish to develop can be seen as a goal. It is amenable to being written down, idealized, verbalized, visualized, emotionalized, and realized. You can design and shape your own character as you go through life by taking control over the things that you think, say, and do. When you repeatedly walk, talk, think, and act in a manner consistent with the values that you wish to program into your personality, you develop new, positive habit patterns of thought and action. You become the person you have imagined yourself to be.

Self-Discipline

Self-discipline is the foundation quality of character. You can have every advantage in life. You can have the best education, and you can memorize every success principle ever discovered. You can have every opportunity in the world opened up to you and have wonderful contacts, but if you lack the self-discipline to master your own will, your own attention, your own thoughts and behaviors, none of them will do you any good.

> With self-discipline, you can do, be, or have, anything that you want.

On the other hand, with self-discipline, carefully developed and regularly practiced, you can do, be, or have, anything that you want. Success is tons of discipline. Perhaps the best definition of self-discipline is the ability to make yourself do what you should do when you should do it, whether you feel like it or not. Only when you can force yourself to do the things that you know are necessary, even when you don't feel like doing them, are you exercising and strengthening your powers of discipline.

I have already said that a positive mental attitude and a sense of inner happiness and personal power comes from a sense of control. When you feel that you are in control of yourself and your life, you feel good about yourself, and you become more capable of doing anything that comes to hand.

A sense of control is the foundation of a healthy personality. Stress and frustration come from feeling out of control of yourself and your life or being controlled by others. Satisfaction and inner strength arise out a feeling that you're in charge of yourself and what happens to you.

The subject of control or what psychologists call the *locus of control*—the place where you feel control is located in your life—is a major issue in psychology today. When you look around you, who or what do you feel is in charge of the critical issues of your life? Many people feel that their boss is in control. Some people feel they're controlled by their bills, their families, or their experiences as children.

> You are in complete control of your life if you choose to be.

Nevertheless, the truth is that you are really in complete control of your life if you choose to be. Self-discipline is the mental quality that enables you to take control of the events in your life, and it is the key to both discipline and personal power.

You can always decide for yourself what you're going to do first, what you're going to do second, and what you're not going to do at all. Your choices about the sequence of events and activities in your life determine everything that happens to you. You are where you are and what you are today because of the choices and decisions that you have made in the past. If you want to improve your life in the future, you can begin at this very moment to make different and better choices.

The wonderful thing about being a free person is that you are always free to choose the sequence of events in your life—what you do and don't do, and in what order. In this freedom lies your ability to sculpt and shape everything that eventually happens to you.

Actions have consequences.

The reality principle says that you can control the action, but the consequences will take on a life of their own. You cannot will the action without simultaneously willing the results.

Many people are confused about this issue. They think that even though they do something that is not particularly productive, they should not have to suffer the consequences of that behavior. But once you have engaged in an action, once you have put the ball into play, the consequences are to a large degree out of your hands.

Here's another important point: inaction is often as important to your future as any particular action that you can take. Whatever has consequences can be considered an action, even if it consists of refraining from doing something. You can set priorities by developing a long time perspective and thinking through the likely consequences of doing or not doing something.

If, for example, you do not continually upgrade your skills, you are setting into motion a series of consequences that will eventually catch up with you and which can cut off major opportunities in the future. A person who goes home at night and watches television is engaging, first, in the action of watching television and, second, in the failure to do something productive. Your time is limited. You can only do a certain number of things each day. Remember the crowding out principle with regard to action and inaction: if you spend an enormous amount of time engaged in high-value activities which move you towards your most important goals, before you know it, the day will be over, and you'll have had no time to spend in activities that do you no good at all.

Unsuccessful people waste their time. Successful people use their time well. In every case, it involves a choice between doing one thing and doing another. Life involves the control that you exert or fail to exert over the sequence of events. Successful people choose to have dinner before dessert. They choose to do what is hard and necessary before they do what is fun and easy. They exert their wills and pay the price of success in advance before engaging in relaxing or amusing activities.

For example, when you get up in the morning, the highest and best use of your time is to mentally and physically exercise and plan and organize the day ahead. But most people get up in the morning, turn on the television or radio, read the newspaper or magazines, drink a little coffee, and roll off to work with barely enough time to get there punctually. Successful people, on the other hand, get up in the morning and they begin immediately to make every minute count.

Whatever you repeat over and over again soon becomes a new habit.

If you came home every night and instead of eating a healthy dinner, you had a big piece of pie with a scoop of ice cream, what would happen to you? How would you feel? What would you be likely to do for the rest of the evening? It would kill your appetite for more nutritious foods. If you did this on a regular basis, you would soon get into the habit of coming home at night and eating pie and ice cream. Afterwards, you would feel tired and sluggish. You would probably sit around and watch television or engage in idle activities. Your physical health would decline. You would get a sugar rush from the pie and ice cream, but afterwards you'd feel depressed and tired.

Many people do something similar with each day.

At the end of their workday, they go to the bar for happy hour or they come home, flip on the television, and begin channel surfing. They look forward to the end of the day so that they can engage in mindless activities. These activities soon become a habit. If someone suggests that they attend a seminar, read a book, or listen to an audio program, they'll come up with all kinds of excuses about being too busy, not having enough time, or being committed to some other activity. They have formed bad habits, which have now become their masters.

Results versus Methods

Many years ago, a life insurance man named Albert E.N. Gray studied successful people for twelve years, looking for what he called "the common denominator of success." His discovery was extremely simple but lastingly important.

He found that the difference between successful people and unsuccessful people was that successful people were more concerned with pleasing *results*. Unsuccessful people, by contrast, were more concerned with pleasing *methods*. Successful people were more concerned with what was likely to happen as a result of their efforts.

Unsuccessful people were more concerned with enjoying the trip, and they didn't give too much thought to what might eventually happen if their main focus was on pleasure on the way through. As Gray put it, "The common denominator of success—the secret of success of every man who has ever been successful—lies in the fact that he formed the habit of doing things that failures don't like to do."

On a similar note, motivational speaker Denis Waitley says that successful people are focused on *goal achieving* while unsuccessful people are focused on *tension relieving*. Now there is a place for tension relieving, but it comes after goal achieving. There is a place for dessert, but it comes after dinner. If you go home and eat a nutritious dinner, your desire for dessert will diminish dramatically. You will eat much less of it. You will have your dessert, but it will be in the proper sequence of events.

It will not become the focus of the meal.

This ability to choose the sequence of events—particularly to do what is hard but necessary and helpful to your future—is totally a matter of self-discipline and willpower. It is your ability to be adamant with yourself and force yourself over and over again to do what is necessary until it becomes a habit.

Successful people have developed the habit of self-discipline. Failures have never developed it. From the days of the ancient Greeks, all of education was character education, and its core was developing within young people the disciplines that would then serve them for the rest of their lives.

Let's say you're not as well-disciplined as you would like to be. What do you do? The answer is simple.

Aristotle dealt with it in the fourth century BC: you behave the way a well-disciplined person behaves. Gradually this behavior becomes a habit, and this habit becomes the virtue you are trying to attain. You can cultivate any or all of the virtues in this manner.

> You become disciplined by behaving the way a well-disciplined person behaves.

Imagine to yourself exactly how you might behave if you were already well disciplined. Dwell on this particular thought, and visualize it regularly. Affirm to yourself, "I am extremely well disciplined." Say this over and over to yourself throughout the day. Most importantly, act as if you already were a highly disciplined person. Carry yourself at every moment as if you were one of the most disciplined people that anyone could meet. Fake it until you make it. Pretend that you are disciplined until this new behavior locks itself into your subconscious mind and you actually become automatically disciplined and controlled in everything you do.

This is not an easy process, but it is eminently doable. We are seeing situations today where young people are taken out of the inner cities after a lifetime of poor schooling, poor parenting, and poor experiences and are joining the armed forces. After two solid years in the armed forces, they're coming out as proud, strong, well-organized, and well-disciplined young people.

Discipline can be trained into you, and you can train it into yourself. The foundation of character is discipline, and your job is to work on yourself to develop it and keep working on it all the days of your life.

When you begin to develop the kinds of discipline that will serve you, don't try to change your whole world at once. Pick one simple discipline and work on that. Every discipline that you practice strengthens every other one. Similarly, every weakness in discipline weakens your discipline in other respects as well, so be careful.

For example, if you decide to get up earlier, discipline yourself to get up fifteen minutes earlier for several days, maybe even several weeks. Do this over and over again until it becomes automatic to get up fifteen to thirty minutes earlier.

Don't try to change the world; just change one thing until you lock it in. Then, using that as a stepping stone, establish another discipline, like getting up fifteen minutes earlier still.

One of the best disciplines is to plan every day in advance, set priorities, and begin each morning with your most important and usually your most difficult task. Once you've begun on this task, discipline yourself to stay with it until it's complete. Make it a habit to handle your tasks singly. Make it a habit to work on the most valuable use of your time and to keep on keeping on until you finish the job.

Courage

Earlier, I talked about the qualities of leaders throughout the ages. I said that in there was one quality that all leaders seem to have in common: *vision*.

There's a second quality all leaders also have in common: *courage*. Winston Churchill once wrote that courage is rightly considered the foremost of the virtues, for upon it all others depend. If vision is the first part of leadership, having the courage to fulfill your vision is the second part. You've heard it said that the road to hell is paved with good intentions. The world is full of people with lofty goals, but there are very few who have the courage, discipline, and willpower to carry them out.

> Courage is considered the foremost of the virtues, for upon it all others depend.

When you live consistently with a virtue like self-discipline and its companion, courage, each time you practice this virtue, you feel stronger and better about yourself. Your self-esteem goes up. You feel more confident and competent. You feel happier and stronger inside. On the other hand, each time you cave in in terms of discipline or courage, your self-esteem goes down. You feel weaker and less confident. You don't like or respect yourself as much.

Becoming personally powerful requires that you live consistently with the highest values you know. They are not only self-reinforcing but self-rewarding. You get an immediate payoff of inner satisfaction each time you force yourself to do what you know you should do, even when you don't feel like it.

I said earlier that the fear of failure is the greatest single obstacle to success.

The antidote to this fear is the courage to act. Courage is so important that, like physical fitness, it requires a variety of exercises to build and maintain it. Of course, you develop courage by facing your fears. Ralph Waldo Emerson wrote, "Do the thing you fear and the death of fear is certain." When you do the what you are afraid of, you take control over both your emotions and your life. You take your attitude from neutral or negative to positive and optimistic.

Systematic Desensitization

As I said earlier, many people fear public speaking, but Toastmasters International has developed a powerful method of teaching public speaking, even to people who are terrified of standing up and speaking in front of others. It is called *systematic desensitization*, and you can use it in many other areas of your life as well.

Systematic desensitization means doing something over and over again until it no longer holds any negative emotion for you. In Toastmasters International, each member is required to stand up and speak, even if for just a few seconds, at every meeting. After several months of weekly meetings, a person who was so terrified that he couldn't lead silent prayer in a phone booth becomes confident about his ability to stand up and speak in front of his peers. Eventually they compete for bigger and longer opportunities to talk on their feet.

I've worked with countless executives who have taken my advice and joined Toastmasters or taken a course from the Dale Carnegie organization. Within six months, they tell me that they're completely different people. They've gone from being shy and self-effacing at meetings to being calm, confident, bold, and even eloquent at expressing their points on their feet, and their careers take off as well.

If you can speak on your feet, you appear to be smarter and more competent than a person who cannot. Many executives, both men and women, have seen their careers take off, their incomes increase, and their responsibilities expand as they face their fears by speaking over and over again until they became very good at it.

In the Serengeti Plains of Africa, zoologists have developed a simple technique to determine which animal in a herd of antelopes is the leader. When a predator approaches and the members of the herd pick up the scent in the wind, they begin drifting in the opposite direction. Soon after, the leader will emerge: he will place himself between the predator and the herd while the herd begins to flee. The leader risking his life with a lion or cheetah that is moving in on the herd will nonetheless stand his ground to buy time for the others to escape.

The leader always turns toward danger.

The leader always turns toward danger. This is as true for human beings as it is for animals. You become a leader to the degree to which you force yourself to turn toward danger. You identify the areas in your life that cause you stress and anxiety. Instead of avoiding them and hoping they will go away, you confront them directly.

The actor Glenn Ford once said that if you do not do the things you fear, the fear controls your life. It's as if the fear were the puppeteer and you were the puppet. If you don't cut the strings that hold you to the fear, it will make you dance emotionally and psychologically. If you let a fear go on for too long, it'll tend to grow and will eventually dominate your thinking.

Each time you think of the fearful situation or person, your heart will beat faster, and your stomach will churn. You'll be unable to sleep well at night. The fear will affect your health, your happiness, and your interactions. Over time, you'll become so preoccupied with the fear-inducing situation that you'll be unable to think of anything else. This is no way to live.

You deal with fear by confronting it. You face the fear, you deal with it, and you put an end to it. When I was a young man and confronted with a lot of fearful situations, I read a quote from Mark Twain: "Courage is not lack of fear or absence of fear. It is mastery of fear, control of fear." The quote had an enormous impact on me.

I realized that we are all afraid of many things. To be afraid is normal and natural. In fact, the more intelligent you are, the greater number of possible fears you'll have, because you'll also have a greater sensitivity to your world and to the possible objects of fear. The only difference between the brave person and the coward is that the brave person confronts the fear and deals with it while the coward turns from the fear and flees from it.

Here's a wonderful thing: when you confront a fear and move toward it, it diminishes and loses its hold over you, but if you back away, it grows larger and soon dominates your thinking and emotions. When you habitually turn toward danger, do the thing you fear, face the fear situation, and move toward it bravely, it grows smaller and smaller. Soon you dominate the fear rather than having it dominate you.

Soon you have a tremendous sense of control.

As I've mentioned, the virtues I set out at the beginning of this chapter are mutually reinforcing, so the quality that you need above all to face your fears is self-discipline. When you discipline yourself to face your fears and act courageously even when you don't feel like it, your fear tends to resolve itself. You feel terrific about yourself; you take full control over the evolution of your own character.

The first part of courage is the courage to launch in the direction of your goal. It is your ability and willingness for you to set a goal and then take the first step in the direction of achieving it.

The Corridor Principle

In a twelve-year study at Babson College, entrepreneurial expert Robert Ronstadt found that the primary difference between those who graduated from the school and went on to build successful businesses and those who did not was that those who built successful businesses were not afraid to launch their businesses before they could ever be guaranteed of any kind of success.

Professor Ronstadt then articulated what has come to be called the *corridor principle*. He said that when you launch toward your goal, however distant, you begin to move down a corridor of time. As you move down this corridor, other doors of opportunity open up on either side of you, but you would not have been in a position to see the other doors of opportunity if you had not been in motion down this psychological corridor toward a goal. And most people who succeed greatly in life succeed in an area completely different from the area in which they started off, but because they were in motion, they saw opportunities and possibilities that would not have been available to them if they had waited until everything was just right, and by the way, everything will never be just right.

The second part of courage is the courage to endure. It is the courage to hang in there. It is the courage to stay the course. It is the courage to persist in the face of all kinds of adversity and self-discipline is the iron quality of character that enables you both to begin and to endure. Self-discipline is the single quality that enables you to develop the high levels of courage that you need to take risks and to move forward in the face of danger and uncertainty. It is self-discipline and the courage that comes from self-discipline that develops personal power within you that enables you to overcome any obstacle in your way.

> ### The Forms of Courage
> 1. To dream big dreams and set big goals
> 2. To make a total commitment
> 3. To move out of your comfort zone
> 4. To take a stand
> 5. To face danger
> 6. To practice zero-based thinking
> 7. To admit you are wrong
> 8. To accept complete responsibility for your life
> 9. To practice courageous patience

The Forms of Courage

There are several forms of courage that you need and which you can develop by practice to achieve the personal greatness that lies within you.

The first form is the courage to dream big dreams and to set big goals. That is where most people come to a halt.

The idea of setting big, challenging, exciting, worthwhile goals is so overwhelming that they quit before they even begin. But this is not for you, so sit down, write out your goals as if anything were possible for you, and never be afraid to dream big dreams.

The second type of courage is the courage to make a total commitment: throwing yourself wholeheartedly into whatever you decide to do. Successful people are living fully engaged and fully involved in their lives and goals. They don't do things by half measures. They may have no guarantees, but they're not afraid to put their whole hearts into their activities. If they fail, they will fail by trying greatly, not by standing on the sidelines, wishing and hoping that things could be just right.

The third type of courage you need is the courage to move out of your comfort zone, to move into your zone of discomfort, where you feel awkward, clumsy, and alone.

As I've already indicated, the comfort zone is one of the greatest enemies of human potential. When people get into a comfort zone, they strive to stay there. Often their whole lives pass them by while they're furnishing and reinforcing their little rut of medium performance. You need the courage to continually move yourself toward your biggest goals and ambitions, and you need to be willing to face discomfort in order to grow.

The fourth type of courage is the courage to take a stand, especially for your values, vision, and beliefs. Stand up for what you believe to be right and for others who espouse those principles. Have the courage to stand foursquare for the highest values that you know. Refuse to compromise your character or your values on the grounds that others may disapprove.

You also need the courage to launch your enterprises in faith with no guarantees of success. As someone once pointed out, if every obstacle had to be overcome first, nothing would ever get done. However, if you look back upon every step forward as a learning experience and every setback as a valuable lesson to make you stronger and better, you'll not be afraid to launch in faith into the unknown. You need the courage to risk failure, to endure constant setbacks, disappointments, and temporary defeats. Realize that failure is an indispensable prerequisite for success. Treat failure as an opportunity to begin again more intelligently.

Again, overcome the fear of failure by doing the things you fear over and over and then by resolving to bounce rather than break when things don't work out for you. The higher and better goals you set for yourself, the more times you'll trip and fall. But as long as you have clear goals, you'll always be failing and falling in a forward direction. You will always be picking yourself up a little closer to the goal than before.

You need the courage to turn continually toward danger. Identify the situations that cause you fear or stress. Examine the worst possible outcome of each. Resolve to accept the worst should it occur, and act to resolve each situation. Refuse to allow a fear situation to remain in your life, dominating your thinking and emotions and holding you back.

You need the courage to continually practice zero-based thinking. Ask, is there anything that you would not get into if you had to do it over again today? Use these words: "Knowing what I now know, do I see anything in my life that I wouldn't start if I had to do it over?" Such situations occur to everyone. If you decide that you wouldn't get into something, your next question is, how do you get out and how fast. You can't make a great life for yourself if there is something that you wouldn't even get into if you had to do it over again. You always know when you are dealing with such a situation: it causes you a great deal of stress.

It preoccupies you continually. It sometimes keeps you awake at night and dominates your conversation. You always know what it is.

When you get new information on any situation that leads to you change your mind about its value, have the courage to admit that you are wrong and you have made a mistake. It's amazing how many people keep themselves locked into a low level of performance because they won't admit that they're not perfect. They will not admit that with the passing of time, something that seemed like a good idea has proven to be a bad one.

Don't be afraid to cut your losses. Don't be afraid to admit that you were wrong and to bail out. Don't be afraid to put one course of action aside and embark on something completely different. This is the mark of courage, personal power, and effective thinking. You need the courage to be willing to make mistakes and learn from them.

All peak performers continually make decisions, make mistakes, learn from them, self-correct, and carry on. Successful people do not necessarily make the right decisions all the time, but they eventually make their decisions right. If they make a mistake, they shrug it off, learn from it as much as possible, and then continue on. You can only learn to succeed by failing and making mistakes. The more you fail and the more mistakes you make, the smarter you are getting, and the more likely you are to succeed eventually.

Have the courage to accept complete responsibility for your life, which means taking ownership for results. Have the courage to refuse to make excuses or defend yourself and to say over and over again, "I am responsible. I am responsible."

When something goes wrong, you immediately become future-oriented and solution-oriented. You say, what do we do from here? What's the next step? What did we learn?

You pick yourself up, extracting the wheat from the situation and throwing away the chaff.

Practice courageous patience. This is a special quality of leadership whereby you remain courageous after you've embarked towards your goal but have not yet seen any results. Many people break and run in the zone between when they begin and when they begin to see a payoff, but this is not for you. Once you've started towards your goal, remain calm, confident, and patient until things begin to happen one way or another.

Persistence

The final kind of courage you need, as I've said before, is the courage to hang in longer than anyone else. Persistence will ultimately guarantee your success. Your ability to persist in the face of anything that the world can throw at you can be your greatest asset. If you refuse to quit, you must ultimately succeed. Just as in baseball, if you keep on swinging, you must ultimately hit a home run.

After decades of studying successful people, I have found one thing for sure: no one was ever defeated until they accepted defeat as a reality. If you persist long enough and hard enough, you must ultimately succeed. No one can ever defeat you but yourself.

When you develop the self-discipline to make yourself do what you should do when you should do it, whether you feel like it or not, and you use this self-discipline to build high levels of courage and persistence, you'll become a powerful individual. You'll soon feel that there is nothing that you cannot accomplish.

Key Points in This Chapter

1. The three essential qualities of success: self-discipline, courage, and persistence.
2. You are in complete control of your life if you choose to be.
3. The reality principle says that you can control the action, but the consequences will take on a life of their own.

4. Successful people are more concerned with pleasing *results*. Unsuccessful people, by contrast, are more concerned with pleasing *methods*.
5. Systematic desensitization means doing something over and over again until it no longer holds any negative emotion for you.
6. You become a leader to the degree to which you force yourself to turn toward danger.
7. Live and practice the nine forms of courage.

twelve

The Keys to Success

Your ability to think big about yourself and your future is the starting point of important achievements. You can accomplish more on the outside than you can imagine yourself capable of on the inside. The more you expand your inner attitudes of mind, the bigger goals and dreams you will set for yourself; the higher standards you aspire to, the more you will accomplish.

Success leaves tracks. It is not an accident. It happens for specific reasons to specific people. Throughout history, countless men and women have started with nothing—sometimes late in life—and gone on to achieve great success. If you want to live the life of which you are capable, you must study other successful people, as we have done throughout this book, and do what they do over and over until you get the same results.

As I've said, self-discipline is the iron quality of character and personal success. You can know everything there is to know on a subject, but until you have the discipline to apply it on a regular basis, it'll do you no good. A person with limited talents, limited resources, and limited contacts can accomplish extraordinary things if they have the willpower to pay the price of success until he achieves it.

Characteristics of High Performance

The Gallup Organization ran a study in which they interviewed 1,500 of the men and women listed in *Who's Who in America*. This is a listing of the most prestigious Americans living today. It includes presidents, senators, and congressmen, plus the heads of major industrial corporations, university presidents, Nobel Prize winners, and many others who have made significant contributions to their worlds. It even includes a high-school football coach who never earned more than $26,000 per year but whose influence on his students was so profound that he turned out champion after champion.

In interviewing these high-performing men and women and the people around them, the researchers developed a profile of high performance. They found that the most successful men and women in America had five qualities in common.

> ### Five Qualities of Successful Individuals
> 1. Common sense
> 2. Self-reliance
> 3. Expertise
> 4. Intelligence
> 5. Result orientation

The first quality they identified was *common sense*. Common sense was defined as a practical objective way of looking at their lives and problems and being able to think them through sensibly and systematically. It was also defined as the ability to have an experience, learn from that experience, and then apply the results of that experience to subsequent experiences. Wisdom enables you to recognize a mistake when you about to make it again.

More importantly, successful people shave had a considerable amount of experience by which they have learned to identify patterns in their work and the world around them.

As a result of this capacity, when they see a new event, it reminds them of a previous situation. They can almost instantly make a correct decision about what is likely to happen and what they should do to avoid danger or to capitalize on opportunity.

Aristotle once wrote that wisdom is an equal measure of experience plus reflection. It is not experiences alone that make you wise; it is the time that you take to reflect on them that enables you to absorb the valuable lessons they offer.

Successful men and women allocate specific times for sitting quietly by themselves and reflecting on what is happening to them. These periods of reflection enable them to integrate their experiences into new patterns.

These new patterns then enable them to think better and more efficiently when they experience future events.

> Wisdom is an equal measure of knowledge
> plus experience plus reflection.

I would add to Aristotle's dictum by saying that today, wisdom is an equal measure of knowledge plus experience plus reflection.

You have to continually take in new knowledge that you can use and compare with your old knowledge and experiences in order to make better decisions for the future. Again, knowledge in every field is doubling every two to three years, so your knowledge of your field must also double every two to three years just for you to stay even. To get ahead, you must study and work on yourself even harder.

For many years, the most successful people were those who had more, and the least successful were those who had less. It was always a contest between the haves and the have-nots.

However, in the information age, when the primary sources of value are knowledge, skill, and the ability to usefully apply them, the major differences are between those who know more and those who know less. High incomes flow to those people who have developed themselves to the point where they can add considerable value in their work. A neurosurgeon earns more than a ditch digger, but it takes fifteen years of study and practice for a person to make a good living as a neurosurgeon. This doesn't mean that the neurosurgeon is a better person than the ditch digger; it just means that the neurosurgeon has invested far more time and effort to develop that knowledge and skill and to attain that level of income.

The website of the Association of Public and Land-Grant Universities offers these facts:
- College graduates are half as likely to be unemployed as their peers who only have a high-school degree.
- Typical earnings for bachelor's degree holders are $40,500, or 86 percent higher than those whose highest degree is a high school diploma.
- College graduates on average make $1.2 million more over their lifetime.

Investment in higher education pays off.

The second quality of high-performing men and women in America identified by the Gallup Organization was *self-reliance*: these people looked to themselves for the solutions to their problems.

They refused to make excuses or blame others. They were highly responsible for themselves in all respects. They didn't expect anyone else to come along and help them. They knew that if they wanted to improve their lives or their work, it was up to them to get busy doing it. They knew that they were where they were and what they were because of themselves; if they wanted things to change, it was up to them to do it.

The interesting thing about self-reliance is that when you make a habit of looking to yourself rather than expecting help from others, others will line up to help you. But if you attempt to get others to help you before you take the first step, people will avoid you at all costs.

The third quality of high performers identified by the Gallup survey was *expertise*. These men and women became well-known for being top performers in their fields.

As a result, they earned the respect and esteem of their colleagues and subordinates as well as of other people within their professions and industries, who could and would help them up the ladder of success.

Your goal is to belong to the top 10 percent of your field. Curiously, the hardest part of becoming a top performers is deciding to do so in the first place. I've worked with hundreds, perhaps thousands, of the top people in every industry. In every case, the turning point in their lives occurred when they made a firm decision and committed themselves to paying whatever price it took to get into the top 10 percent.

Once you get into the top 10 percent, you will find that your life is better than you can imagine today.

It doesn't matter if it takes a week, a month, a year, or several years; it's worth the price. You'll enjoy much higher levels of self-esteem and personal pride. You'll have a far higher standard of living. Perhaps most important of all, you will have the respect and esteem of the top people around you.

The fourth quality identified in the Gallup study was *intelligence*. Intelligence was defined in three ways. The first was simply a matter of IQ: a person was intelligent because they got good grades in school, but this was not the most important part. Another aspect of intelligence is *emotional intelligence*: the ability to interact effectively with other people, especially to empathize with them and so enroll them in helping you to achieve your goals. A brilliant person without empathy will have limited career success.

The third and perhaps the most important definition of intelligence is that it is a way of acting. If you act intelligently, you are smart. If you act stupidly, you are stupid, irrespective of your IQ.

> An intelligent way of acting is one that moves you toward your goals.

What, then, is an intelligent way of acting? That's easy: it moves you closer to one of your own self-determined goals. Everything that you do that moves you toward achieving what you have decided is important to you is an intelligent act. On the other hand, every time you do something that is inconsistent with your own goals or moves you away from them, you are behaving stupidly. Most people don't understand that if their goal is to be healthy, trim, and fit, every time they refrain from exercising or overeating, they are behaving stupidly by their own definition of what they want.

If your goal is to be one of the top people in your field but you spend endless hours surfing the Internet and driving around listening to music instead of studying your craft, you are behaving stupidly.

The final ingredient of success possessed by the highest performing people in America was found to be *result orientation*. I'll come back to it again below.

My big breakthrough in understanding success came many years ago, when I realized that it was largely a matter of how you feel about yourself. If you feel terrific about yourself, you'll be more willing to take the necessary risks that move you toward your goals. The higher your level of self-esteem and self-regard, the more courage and confidence you will have, and the more willing you will be to dream big dreams and set big goals.

Sometimes people ask me about luck. They're convinced that it plays a major role in success. They feel that some people have it and some people don't. They try to convince me that a person gets to the top of their field largely as a result of getting lucky breaks (of which they themselves have been deprived). I've studied luck for many years. My conclusion is that it is based on probabilities. Hence the more things you do that are likely to help you to succeed, the more likely you are to do the right thing at the right time.

It is not a matter of luck. It is a matter of clear design. If you were throwing darts at a dartboard even in a darkened room, you would eventually hit the board; if you threw enough darts, you would eventually hit a bull's-eye. However, if the light were on and you could see the dartboard clearly and you had ample time to practice and an unlimited supply of darts, it would dramatically shorten the time it would take you to shoot a bull's-eye. (Of course when you did, everyone would exclaim how lucky you were.)

The Great Life

Your reason for reading this book—and your aim in life—is not just to live but to live greatly. You aim to do something wonderful. You want to accomplish extraordinary things. You don't go out and have a great life; you make it a great life.

You recognize yourself as the primary creative force in your own life, and you make it into what you want it to be.

> ### The GREAT Acronym
> G: goal orientation
> R: result orientation
> E: excellence orientation
> A: action orientation
> T: time orientation

The word *great* has five letters: G-R-E-A-T. This can be used as an acronym standing for the five keys to success. I've discussed them throughout this book, but I want to touch on them briefly to give you a clear track to run on from this point forward.

Goal Orientation

The first letter of the word, G, stands for *goal orientation*. All high-performing men and women are extremely goal-oriented. They have a clear vision of their ideal futures. They have written goals and written plans to accomplish them. They review their goals on a regular basis. They read books, and they study goal setting so that they can become more and more skilled at it.

They recognize that you cannot hit a target that you can't see.

The keys to goal setting are simple. To repeat: first, decide exactly what you want. Second, write it down clearly and in detail. Third, set a deadline, and if it's a large goal, set subdeadlines for it. Fourth, make a plan: a list of every single thing that you could think of that you could possibly do to achieve the goal. Then organize your list of activities in terms of time and priority. What should you do first, and what is most important?

Sixth, take action towards your goal. Do something, anything, that moves you one step ahead. As the Chinese sage Lao Tzu said, a journey of a thousand leagues begins with a single step.

Seventh, make a total commitment to your goal. Resolve that once you have started towards it, you'll never, never give up.

Those seven steps can be repeated over and over again. When you finish this book, take out a pad of paper and write out the goals that you want to achieve. Organize them by priority. Ask yourself, "If I could only achieve one goal on this list, which would contribute the most to my life?"

A key part of goal setting is to be clear about the outcome you desire but to be flexible about the process. Once you have programmed a goal into your subconscious and superconscious minds, remarkable things will happen to you, many of them completely unexpected. You must be ready to change your direction when a new opportunity opens up.

Flexibility is the principal quality you'll require to thrive in the years ahead. You must be willing to change course, reconsider your direction, and try something completely different on the way to your goals. But as long as your goals are clear, they will materialize exactly when you're ready for them.

Result Orientation

The second letter in the word *great* is the letter R. R stands for *result orientation*. High-performing men and women get the results they are responsible for. They have developed the ability to do the job that others are counting on them to do.

Success and failure in our society today depend solely on a person's ability to deliver. For most of human history, people were manual laborers. They worked with their muscles and by the sweat of their brow. In the last few decades, we have made a dramatic shift from manpower to mind power. As of April 2023, 76 percent of all people in our society were earning their living with their minds, not their muscles. Today you are a knowledge worker. A knowledge worker is a person who must first decide what is to be done before they become involved in how it is to be done.

You are the president of your own personal services corporation. You are the chief executive officer of a company with one employee: yourself. Your primary job is to sell the services of your corporation for the best combination of rewards and opportunities. You must be continually thinking how you can apply your special knowledge and experience in the marketplace to achieve the highest return for yourself. Your most valuable asset, the major source of cash flow for your company, is your earning ability: the ability to utilize your knowledge and skill to bring about results others will pay for. This earning ability is gradually becoming obsolete every day, every week, every month. You must therefore continually upgrade your earning ability if you want to continue to earn the kind of money that you have set as your goal. Your most precious resource is your time, and the best investment of your time is to continually increase your earning ability.

Every effort that you make to upgrade your knowledge and skills adds to your ability to earn more money and increases your flexibility. It makes you more capable of doing more different and valuable jobs for more different customers or employers under more different circumstances.

Many people today are upset because they don't earn more money or, even worse, because they get laid off from jobs that they've had for some time. They think it is up to the company or society to create highly paid jobs and keep them employed. But only you can create a highly paid job. You do so by becoming highly productive. No one else can do this for you. The company merely hires your services and combines it with the services of others to produce a product that the market will pay for.

Your job is to make sure that your contribution to these services is worth every penny, and more, that they pay.

The primary reason for failure in a market-based economy is low levels of productivity, usually combined with time wastage. This is why it is so important to continually focus on high-value activities, work on key result areas, define and determine your critical success factors, and plan to become excellent in each one of them.

Work all the time you work. Work time is not playtime. Let the other people around you socialize and go out for long lunches and coffee breaks. Your job, your goal, is to be the best you can be and to get real results for your organization. More than perhaps any other single factor, developing a reputation for hard work will bring you to the attention of people who can help you.

Excellence Orientation

The third letter in the word *great* E stands for *excellence orientation*. A wise man once told me that the key to success in any field is to get good, get better, and be the best. When you resolve to be the best at what you do, you will find that there is very little competition. When you decide to do more than you are paid for or to go the extra mile, you will find that there is very little competition as well. There are never any traffic jams on the extra mile.

> There are never any traffic jams on the extra mile.

The wonderful thing about working all out, putting your whole heart into what you do, and greatly exceeding what your company expects of you is that it puts you on the side of the angels. Not only do you feel terrific about yourself, but you earn the high regard of others.

You become better and better in your field and increase your competence and your earning ability immeasurably.

Many years ago, when I was working for a very successful businessman, I used to put in ten-, twelve- and even fourteen-hour days. Sometimes I was away from home for several days and even weekends. When the other people in the company asked me why I worked so hard when I wasn't getting paid any more than they were, I couldn't answer them. Later I realized that I was actually taking advantage of my boss. I was using the doors of opportunity he opened for me to develop my skills at a far more rapid rate than the others in the company. Before the dust had settled, I was making more money than any of them. I had more responsibilities. I had a larger staff and a higher salary than any of the people I started with.

By taking advantage of my employer (as you can do), I accelerated my growth and my career by several years. Do the same thing. Remember that excellence is a journey, not a destination. It's a moving target. Moreover, your weakest vital skill usually sets the height at which you can use all your other skills, so go to someone you trust and ask them if they see any weaknesses in your performance. If you're in sales, ask your manager or even one of your customers. Take people out with you and have them sit and observe your work; have people comment on what they see or fail to see. It's almost impossible for you to get better by yourself or to identify your areas of weakness without input from others. As Ken Blanchard, author of *The One Minute Manager*, says, feedback is the breakfast of champions.

Read everything you possibly can about your field.

If anything, dedicate yourself to overlearning. You should know deep down inside that you'll seldom meet anyone who knows as much about your business as you do. At one point, Ben Feldman was the top salesman in the world, according to *The Guinness Book of Records*, yet he was still studying two hours every night to keep on top of changes in his field. You should do the same.

Continually invest in yourself. Sometimes you hear people complain that education is expensive. If they think education is expensive, they should try ignorance.

There's nothing worse than working ten or twenty extra years to achieve the same level of income that you could have achieved years earlier if you had taken the time to learn your craft and become excellent at it at an earlier age.

> If you think education is expensive, try ignorance.

In every manufacturing process today, there are by-products that are usually thrown away. However, in an age of conservation, some companies are finding new ways to take these by-products and turn them into new products. Sometimes these by-products become more profitable than the main product itself.

In your work life, the by-products of your day-to-day activities are your spare time. It is often your judicious use of spare time, the by-products of your day that will largely determine your success or failure. Use your time wisely to continually upgrade your skills and your earning ability and to become excellent at what you do.

Action Orientation

The fourth letter in the word *great*, A, stands for *action orientation*. High performers are intensely action-oriented. It's probably the number one quality of success. The more different things you do and the faster you do them, the more you learn and the better you get.

The big killer of human potential is procrastination: putting off big, important tasks until later and finally never getting to them at all. Procrastination is a habit based on inertia or fear. You can and must get over it.

Becoming intensely action oriented requires you to make a habit of deciding what you want to do and then moving quickly before you have time to think about it or to be afraid.

One of my favorite rules for success is this: act boldly, and unseen forces will come to your aid.

When you act boldly, when you seize the initiative and continue acting, you develop a sense of forward momentum that keeps you going long after the average person has quit.

Today time is the single most valuable factor in production. Saving time is the essence of everything you do to improve your effectiveness and productivity, and saving time requires that you move quickly when opportunity presents itself. You develop a sense of urgency. You do it now. You set clear goals; you determine the specific results you need to get to achieve the goals. You dedicate yourself to becoming very good at what you do, and you take continuous action in the direction of your dreams.

Time Orientation

The final letter in the word great is the letter T, which stands for *time orientation*. Top people give a lot of thought to how they use their time. They plan it and allocate it carefully.

They make sure they're using it on their highest-value activities. They take a lot of time to stand back and look at where they're going to get the necessary minutes and hours to perform their most important tasks.

Time management allows you to control the sequence of events in your work. It allows you to determine what to do first, what to do second, and what to do not at all. It gives you a tremendous sense of control—and remember, you are always free to choose the sequence of events. You're always free to choose what you do and what you don't do, and those choices will determine everything that happens to you.

You cannot save time. You can only spend it differently.

You cannot save time. You can only spend it differently. You can only reallocate time away from low-value activities toward high-value activities. You can reallocate it away from idle socializing toward the activities that really make a positive difference in your life.

The most important part of time management is your ability to set priorities. Apply the 80/20 rule to everything you do, and work continuously on only those items in the top 20 percent that represent 80 percent of the value.

Time management is really life management. When we talk about saving time, we're really talking about saving life. You read, listen to audio programs, take courses, and continually upgrade your skills because knowledge and information represent condensed time. It can save you weeks and months of hard work when you become better and better at what you do. Investing in yourself is one of the highest payoffs of your time that you can engage in.

There's an old proverb that says that if you eat a live frog first thing when you get up in the morning, you can go through the day with the confidence of knowing that that is the worst thing that could possibly happen to you.

By the same token, if you get up each morning and you immediately begin work on the biggest, most difficult, and most important task facing you, and you discipline yourself to work at it single-mindedly until it's complete, you'll have the satisfaction of knowing that you are on top of your work and on top of your life.

As we conclude, I want to remind you that we are living in the greatest time in all of human history. There are more opportunities and possibilities available to you today than ever before. If you commit yourself to dreaming big dreams, getting continually better at what you do, working on your high-priority tasks continually and to never, never giving up, there is virtually nothing in the world that you cannot accomplish.

Thank you for reading this book. I wish you the very best of health, happiness, and success in the months and years ahead. Please take the practical ideas contained here and apply them to your life. Make a list of activities today. Organize the list by priority, select the most important thing that you can possibly do, and every day, get up and eat that frog. Good luck.

Key Points in This Chapter

1. Five qualities of successful individuals: common sense, self-reliance, expertise, intelligence, and result orientation.
2. Successful people allocate time for sitting quietly and reflecting.
3. Investment in higher education pays off.
4. Your goal is to belong to the top 10 percent of your field.

5. Emotional intelligence is the ability to interact and empathize with others.
6. The GREAT acronym: goal orientation, result orientation, excellence orientation, action orientation, time orientation.
7. Putting your whole heart into what you do puts you on the side of the angels.
8. Time is the single most valuable factor in production.

www.ingramcontent.com/pod-product-compliance
Lightning Source LLC
Chambersburg PA
CBHW072153070526
44585CB00015B/1117